[redacted]

CHRIST in His SANCTUARY

A Compilation from the Writings
of
Ellen G. White

"The subject of the sanctuary and the investigative judgment should be clearly understood by the people of God."—*The Great Controversy,* page 488.

"I know that the sanctuary question stands in righteousness and truth, just as we have held it for so many years. It is the enemy that leads minds off on sidetracks. He is pleased when those who know the truth become engrossed in collecting scriptures to pile around erroneous theories, which have no foundation in truth. The scriptures thus used are misapplied; they were not given to substantiate error, but to strengthen truth."—*Gospel Workers,* page 303.

PACIFIC PRESS PUBLISHING ASSOCIATION
Mountain View, California Oshawa, Ontario

[redacted]

Contents

Litho in United States of America

Library of Congress Catalog Card No. 70-94869

Six printings, 75,000
ISBN 0-8163-0128-X

The Sanctuary Truth

An Introduction*

Writing of what must be accomplished by the emerging Seventh-day Adventist Church before the Lord shall come, Ellen G. White in 1883 said:

"The minds of believers were to be directed to the heavenly sanctuary, where Christ had entered to make atonement for His people."—*Selected Messages,* Bk. 1, p. 67.

In a crisis in 1906, in which certain of the basic teachings of Seventh-day Adventists were threatened, she wrote:

"The correct understanding of the ministration in the heavenly sanctuary is the foundation of our faith."—*Evangelism,* page 221.

The End of the 2300 Days

Among the prophecies forming the foundation of the advent awakening of the 1830's and the early 1840's was the prophecy of Daniel 8:14: "Unto two thousand and three hundred days; then shall the sanctuary be cleansed." Ellen White, who passed through the experience, explains concerning the application of this prophecy:

"In common with the rest of the Christian world, Adventists then held that the earth, or some portion of it, was the sanctuary. They understood that the cleansing of the sanctuary was the

*An introductory chapter prepared in the office of the Ellen G. White Estate, providing the historical setting for the E. G. White chapters and other of her materials selected for the study of the sanctuary truth as understood and taught by Seventh-day Adventists.

purification of the earth by the fires of the last great day, and that this would take place at the second advent. Hence the conclusion that Christ would return to the earth in 1844."—*The Great Controversy*, page 409.

This prophetic period came to its close on October 22, 1844. The disappointment to those who expected to meet their Lord on that day was great. Hiram Edson, a careful Bible student in mid-New York State, describes what took place among the company of believers of which he was a part:

"Our expectations were raised high, and thus we looked for our coming Lord until the clock tolled twelve at midnight. The day had then passed, and our disappointment had become a certainty. Our fondest hopes and expectations were blasted, and such a spirit of weeping came over us as I never experienced before. It seemed that the loss of all earthly friends could have been no comparison. We wept and wept, till the day dawn. . . .

"I mused in my heart, saying: 'My advent experience has been the brightest of all my Christian experience. . . . Has the Bible proved a failure? Is there no God, no heaven, no golden city, no Paradise? Is all this but a cunningly devised fable? Is there no reality to our fondest hopes and expectations?' . . .

"I began to feel there might be light and help for us in our distress. I said to some of the brethren: 'Let us go to the barn.' We entered the granary, shut the doors about us, and bowed before the Lord. We prayed earnestly, for we felt our necessity. We continued in earnest prayer until the witness of the Spirit was given that our prayers were accepted, and that light should be given—our disappointment explained, made clear and satisfactory.

"After breakfast I said to one of my brethren, 'Let us go and see and encourage some of our brethren.' We started, and while passing through a large field, I was stopped about midway of the field. Heaven seemed open to my view, and I saw distinctly and clearly that instead of our High Priest coming out of the most holy place of the heavenly sanctuary to this earth on the tenth day of the seventh month, at the end of the 2300 days, He, for the first time, entered on that day into the second apartment of that sanctuary, and that He had a work to perform in the most holy place before coming to the earth; that He came to the marriage, or in other words, to the Ancient of Days, to receive a kingdom, dominion, and glory; and that we must wait for His return from the wedding. And my mind was directed to the tenth chapter of Revelation, where I could see the vision had spoken and did not lie."—Unpublished manuscript published in part in the *Review and Herald*, June 23, 1921.

There followed a careful investigation of the scriptures that touched on this subject—particularly those in Hebrews—by Hiram Edson and two close associates, Dr. F. B. Hahn, a physician, and O. R. L. Crosier, a teacher. The result of this joint study was written up by Crosier and was published, first in *The Day Dawn*, a paper of limited circulation, and then in rewritten and enlarged form in a special issue of the *Day-Star*, on February 7, 1846. This was a more widely read Adventist journal, published at Cincinnati, Ohio. Through this medium it reached a number of the disappointed Advent believers. The rather lengthy presentation, well supported by Scripture, brought hope and courage to their hearts as it clearly showed that the sanctuary to be cleansed at the end of the 2300 days is in heaven, and not on earth, as they had believed earlier.

Ellen G. White, in a statement written on April 21, 1847, declared in endorsement of the Crosier article on the sanctuary question:

"The Lord showed me in vision, more than one year ago, that Brother Crosier had the true light, on the cleansing of the sanctuary, etc.; and that it was His will, that Brother Crosier should write out the view which he gave us in the *Day-Star Extra*, February 7, 1846. I feel fully authorized by the Lord, to recommend that Extra, to every saint."—*A Word to the Little Flock*, page 12.

At a later time she wrote of the rapid development of doctrinal understanding which followed the disappointment:

"The passing of the time in 1844 was a period of great events, opening to our astonished eyes the cleansing of the sanctuary transpiring in heaven, and having decided relation to God's people upon the earth." *Manuscript* 13, 1889, published in *Counsels to Writers and Editors,* page 30.

A Truth Established by the Witness of the Holy Spirit

The visions given to Ellen White, while not running ahead of Bible study, confirmed the soundness of the position that an important phase of Christ's ministry in the heavenly sanctuary was entered upon on October 22, 1844. Gradually the breadth and depth of the subject opened before the Advent believers. Looking back on the experience in later years, she recalled their study and the manifest evidences of God's guiding hand:

"Many of our people do not realize how firmly the foundation of our faith has been laid. My husband, Elder Joseph Bates, Father Pierce,* Elder [Hiram] Edson, and others who were keen, noble, and true, were among those who, after the passing of the time in 1844, searched for the truth as for hidden treasure. I met with them, and we studied and prayed earnestly. Often we remained together until late at night, and sometimes through the entire night, praying for light and studying the Word. Again and again these brethren came together to study the Bible, in order that they might know its meaning, and be prepared to teach it with power. When they came to the point in their study where they said, "We can do nothing more," the Spirit of the Lord would come upon me, I would be taken off in vision, and a clear explanation of the passages we had been studying would be given me, with instruction as to how we were to labor and teach effectively. Thus light was given that helped us to understand the scriptures in regard to Christ, His mission, and His priesthood. A line of truth extending from that time to the time when we shall

---

*Older brethren among the pioneers are here thus reminiscently referred to. "Father Pierce" was Stephen Pierce, who served in ministerial and administrative work in the early days.

enter the City of God, was made plain to me, and I gave to others the instruction that the Lord had given me.

"During this whole time I could not understand the reasoning of the brethren. My mind was locked, as it were, and I could not comprehend the meaning of the scriptures we were studying. This was one of the greatest sorrows of my life. I was in this condition of mind until all the principal points of our faith were made clear to our minds, in harmony with the Word of God. The brethren knew that when not in vision, I could not understand these matters, and they accepted as light direct from heaven the revelations given."—*Selected Messages,* Bk. 1, pp. 206, 207.

The realization that Christ had entered the most holy place in the heavenly sanctuary to begin His closing ministry in our behalf, typified in the sanctuary service observed by Israel of old, solemnized the hearts of our pioneer Adventists. The truths were so clear, so grand, so vital, that it was difficult to sense that upon them rested the responsibility of imparting this light to others. Ellen White wrote of the certainty of their position:

"We are to be established in the faith, in the light of the truth given us in our early experience. At that time one error after another pressed in upon us; ministers and doctors brought in new doctrines. We would search the Scriptures with much prayer, and the Holy Spirit would bring the truth to our minds. Sometimes whole nights would be devoted to searching the Scriptures, and earnestly asking God for guidance. Companies of devoted men and women assembled for this purpose. The power of God would come upon me, and I was enabled clearly to define what is truth and what is error.

"As the points of our faith were thus established, our feet were placed upon a solid foundation. We accepted the truth point by point, under the demonstration of the Holy Spirit. I would be taken off in vision, and explanations would be given me. I was given illustrations of heavenly things, and of the sanctuary, so that we were placed where light was shining on us in clear, distinct rays.

"I know that the sanctuary question stands in righteousness and truth, just as we have held it for so many years."—*Gospel Workers,* pages 302, 303.

The pioneers of the movement saw the sanctuary truth as basic to the whole structure of Seventh-day Adventist doctrine. James White, in 1850, republished the essential portions of the first presentation of the subject by O. R. L. Crosier, and commented:

"The subject of the sanctuary should be carefully examined, as it lies at the foundation of our faith and hope."—*The Advent Review* (special combined number).

The Sanctuary and the Sabbath

It was in the setting of a view of the heavenly sanctuary that the Sabbath truth was confirmed in the vision given to Ellen White on April 3, 1847, at the Howland home in Topsham, Maine. Of this she writes:

"We felt an unusual spirit of prayer. And as we prayed the Holy Ghost fell upon us. We were very happy. Soon I was lost to earthly things and was wrapped in a vision of God's glory. I saw an angel flying swiftly to me. He quickly carried me from the earth to the Holy City. In the city I saw a temple, which I entered. I passed through a door before I came to the first veil. This veil was raised, and I passed into the holy place. Here I saw the altar of incense, the candlestick with seven lamps, and the table on which was the shewbread. After viewing the glory of the holy, Jesus raised the second veil and I passed into the holy of holies.

"In the holiest I saw an ark; on the top and sides of it was purest gold. On each end of the ark was a lovely cherub, with its wings spread out over it. Their faces were turned toward each other, and they looked downward. Between the angels was a golden censer. Above the ark, where the angels stood, was an exceeding bright glory, that appeared like a throne where God dwelt. Jesus stood by the ark, and as the saints' prayers came up to Him, the incense in the censer would smoke, and He would offer up their prayers with the smoke of the incense to His Father. In the ark was the golden pot of manna, Aaron's rod that budded, and the tables of stone which folded together like a book. Jesus opened them, and I saw the Ten Commandments written on them with the finger of God. On one table were four, and on the other six. The four on the first table shone brighter than the other six. But the fourth, the Sabbath commandment, shone above them all; for the Sabbath was set apart to be kept in honor of God's holy name. The holy Sabbath looked glorious —a halo of glory was all around it. I saw that the Sabbath commandment was not nailed to the cross. If it was, the other nine commandments were; and we are at liberty to break them all, as well as to break the fourth. I saw that God had not changed the Sabbath, for He never changes."—*Early Writings,* pages 32, 33.

The Sanctuary Truth Under Fire

While there were those who saw clearly the binding claims of God's law and began to observe the Seventh-day Sabbath as set forth in the law of God, they encountered strong opposition. Of this and the reasons for it, Ellen White explains:

"Many and earnest were the efforts made to overthrow their faith. None could fail to see that if the earthly sanctuary was a figure or pattern of the heavenly, the law deposited in the ark on earth was an exact transcript of the law in the ark in heaven; and that an acceptance of the truth concerning the heavenly sanctuary involved an acknowledgment of the claims of God's law, and the obligation of the Sabbath of the fourth commandment. Here was the secret of the bitter and determined opposition to the harmonious exposition of the Scriptures that revealed the ministration of Christ in the heavenly sanctuary."—*The Great Controversy,* page 435.

It is little wonder that those in subsequent years defecting from the Seventh-day Adventist Church should make the sanctuary truth a point of opposition. It was so with Elders Snook and Brinkerhof, conference officers in Iowa, who withdrew in the middle 1860's, and with D. M. Canright, an influential minister, who left the Seventh-day Adventist Church in 1887 to become a bitter enemy and critic. Nor is it strange that the pantheistic views at the turn of the century, espoused and advocated by both medical and ministerial workers, should strike directly at this fundamental doctrine. It was in this setting that Ellen White in warning words wrote on November 20, 1905:

"To those medical missionaries and ministers who have been drinking in the scientific sophistries and bewitching fables against which you have been warned, I would say, Your souls are in peril. The world must know where you are standing and where Seventh-day Adventists are standing. God calls for all who have accepted these soul-destroying delusions no longer to halt between two opinions. If the Lord be God, follow Him.

"Satan, with all his host is on the battlefield. Christ's soldiers are now to rally round the bloodstained banner of Emmanuel. In the name of the Lord, leave the black banner of the prince of darkness, and take your position with the Prince of heaven.

" 'He that hath ears to hear, let him hear.' Read your Bibles. From higher ground, under the instruction given me of God, I present these things before you. The time is near when the deceptive powers of satanic agencies will be fully developed. On one side is Christ, who has been given all power in heaven and earth. On the other side is Satan, continually exercising his power to allure, to deceive with strong, spiritualistic sophistries, to remove God out of the place that He should occupy in the minds of men.

"Satan is striving continually to bring in fanciful suppositions in regard to the sanctuary, degrading the wonderful representations of God and the ministry of Christ for our salvation into something that suits the carnal mind. He removes its presiding power from the hearts of believers, and supplies its place with fantastic theories invented to make void the truths of the atonement, and destroy our confidence in the doctrines which we have held sacred since the third angel's message was first given. Thus he would rob us of our faith in the very message that has made us a separate people, and has given character and power to our work."—*Special Testimonies,* Series B, No. 7, pp. 16, 17.

It was in the setting of this pantheistic crisis that Ellen White, attending the General Conference session of 1905, declared in words significant to us today:

"In the future, deception of every kind is to arise, and we want solid ground for our feet. We want solid pillars for the building. Not one pin is to be removed from that which the Lord has established. The enemy will bring in false theories, such as the doctrine that there is no sanctuary. This is one of the points on which there will be a departing from the faith. Where shall we find safety unless it be in the truths that the Lord has been giving for the last fifty years?"—*Counsels to Writers and Editors,* page 53.

The pantheistic views, so earnestly advocated by some, Ellen White declared, would "do away with God" (*Special Testimonies,* Series B, No. 7, p. 16) and invalidate the sanctuary truth.

At about the same time one of our ministers, whom we will identify as "Elder G," espoused the view that when Christ went back to heaven after his ministry on earth, He went into the presence of God, and that where God is, must be the most holy place, therefore on October 22, 1844, there was no entering into the most holy place in the heavenly sanctuary as we believed and taught. These two concepts, both of which struck at the doctrine of the sanctuary as we held it, led Ellen White several times to refer to the soundness and integrity of this point of faith. In 1904 she wrote:

"They (the children of God) will not, by their words and acts, lead anyone to doubt in regard to the distinct personality of God, or in regard to the sanctuary and its ministry.

"We all need to keep the subject of the sanctuary in mind. God forbid that the clatter of words coming from human lips should lessen the belief of our people in the truth that there is a sanctuary in heaven, and that a pattern of this sanctuary was once built on this earth. God desires His people to become familiar with this pattern, keeping ever before their minds the heavenly sanctuary, where God is all and in all. We must keep our minds braced by prayer and a study of God's Word, that we may grasp these truths."—E. G. White *Letter* 233, 1904.

Points Sustained Only by Misused Scriptures

Writing particularly of "Elder G's" work in undermining confidence in the sanctuary truth in 1905, Ellen White pointed out the unsoundness of his use of Scripture evidence and the dependability of our understanding of the sanctuary truth. This is what she said:

"I have been pleading with the Lord for strength and wisdom to reproduce the writings of the witnesses who were confirmed in the faith and in the early history of the message. After the passing of the time in 1844 they received the light and walked in the light, and when the men claiming to have new light would come in with their wonderful messages regarding various points of Scripture, we had, through the moving of the Holy Spirit, testimonies right to the point, which cut off the influence of such messages as Elder G has been devoting his time to presenting. This poor man has been working decidedly against the truth that the Holy Spirit has confirmed.

"When the power of God testifies as to what is truth, that truth is to stand forever as the truth. No after suppositions contrary to the light God has given are to be entertained. Men will arise with interpretations of Scripture which are to them truth, but which are not truth. The truth for this time God has given us as a foundation for our faith. He Himself has taught us what is truth. One will arise, and still another, with new light, which contradicts the light that God has given under the demonstration of His Holy Spirit. A few are still alive who passed through the experience gained in the establishment of this truth. God has graciously spared their lives to repeat, and repeat till the close of their lives, the experience through which they passed even as did John the apostle till the very close of his life. And the standard-bearers who have fallen in death are to speak through the reprinting of their writings. I am instructed that thus their voices are to be heard. They are to bear their testimony as to what constitutes the truth for this time.

"We are not to receive the words of those who come with a message that contradicts the special points of our faith. They gather together a mass of Scripture, and pile it as proof around their asserted theories. This has been done over and over again during the past fifty years. And while the Scriptures are God's Word, and are to be respected, the application of them, if such application moves one pillar from the foundation that God has sustained these fifty years, is a great mistake. He who makes such an application knows not the wonderful demonstration of the Holy Spirit that gave power and force to the past messages that have come to the people of God.

"Elder G's proofs are not reliable. If received, they would destroy the faith of God's people in the truth that has made us what we are.

"We must be decided on this subject; for the points that he is trying to prove by Scripture, are not sound. They do not prove that the past experience of God's people was a fallacy. We had the truth; we were directed by the angels of God. It was under the guidance of the Holy Spirit that the presentation of the sanctuary question was given. It is eloquence for everyone to keep silent in regard to the features of our faith in which they acted no part. God never contradicts Himself. Scripture proofs are misapplied if forced to testify to that which is not true. Another and still another will arise and bring in supposedly great light, and make their assertions. But we stand by the old landmarks."—*Selected Messages*, Bk. 1, pp. 160-162.

The Reality of the Heavenly Sanctuary Affirmed

Repeatedly we find in the Ellen G. White writings statements on the reality of the heavenly sanctuary, its furnishings, and its ministry. One such was penned in the 1880's as she described the experience of the Advent believers following the disappointment:

"In their investigation they learned, that the earthly sanctuary, built by Moses at the command of God, according to the pattern shown him in the mount, was 'a figure for the time then present, in which were offered both gifts and sacrifices;' that its two holy places were 'patterns of things in the heavens;' that Christ, our great High Priest, is 'a minister of the sanctuary, and of the true tabernacle, which the Lord pitched, and not man.' . . .

"The sanctuary in heaven, in which Jesus ministers in our behalf, is the great original, of which the sanctuary built by Moses was a copy. . . .

"The matchless splendor of the earthly tabernacle reflected to human vision the glories of that heavenly temple where Christ our forerunner ministers for us before the throne of God.

"As the sanctuary on earth had two apartments, the holy and the most holy, so there are two holy places in the sanctuary in heaven. And the ark containing the law of God, the altar of incense, and other instruments of service found in the sanctuary below, have also their counterpart in the sanctuary above. In holy vision the apostle John was permitted to enter heaven, and he there beheld the candlestick and the altar of incense, and as 'the temple of God was opened,' he beheld also 'the ark of His testament.' [Rev. 4:5; 8:3; 11:19.]

"Those who were seeking for the truth found indisputable proof of the existence of a sanctuary in heaven. Moses made the earthly sanctuary after a pattern which was shown him. Paul declares that that pattern was the true sanctuary which is in heaven. John testifies that he saw it in heaven."—*Spirit of Prophecy,* Vol. IV, pp. 260, 261.

Earlier she had written with emphasis on the furniture:

"I was also shown a sanctuary upon the earth containing two apartments. It resembled the one in heaven, and I was told that it was a figure of the heavenly. The furniture of the first apartment of the earthly sanctuary was like that in the first apartment of the heavenly. The veil was lifted, and I looked into the holy of holies, and saw that the furniture was the same as in the most holy place in the heavenly sanctuary."—*Early Writings,* pages 252, 253.

The Ark and the Law in the Heavenly Sanctuary

On different occasions she spoke and wrote of the ark in the most holy place in the heavenly sanctuary. One such statement was made in a sermon preached in Orebro, Sweden, in 1886.

"I warn you, Do not place your influence against God's commandments. That law is just as Jehovah wrote it in the temple of heaven. Man may trample upon its copy here below, but the original is kept in the ark of God in heaven; and on the cover of this ark, right above that law, is the mercy seat. Jesus stands right there before that ark to mediate for man."—Ellen G. White Comments, *SDA Bible Commentary,* Vol. 1, p. 1109.

And in 1903 she again wrote of the reality of the heavenly sanctuary:

"I could say much regarding the sanctuary; the ark containing the law of God; the cover of the ark, which is the mercy seat; the angels at either end of the ark; and other things connected with the heavenly sanctuary and with the great day of atonement. I could say much regarding the mysteries of heaven; but my lips are closed. I have no inclination to try to describe them."—Ellen G. White *Letter* 253, 1903.

Last-day Delusions Will Involve Vital Truth

It is clear that our adversary, Satan, will try to unsettle the faith of God's people in the doctrine of the sanctuary in these "latter days." Ellen White wrote:

"The Saviour foretold that in the latter days false prophets would appear, and draw away disciples after them; and also that those who in this time of peril should stand faithful to the truth that is specified in the book of Revelation, would have to meet doctrinal errors so specious that, if it were possible, the very elect would be deceived.

"God would have every true sentiment prevail. Satan can skillfully play the game of life with many souls, and he acts in a most underhanded, deceptive manner to spoil the faith of the people of God and to discourage them. . . . He works today as he worked in heaven—to divide the people of God in the very last stage of this earth's history. He seeks to create dissension, and to arouse contention and discussion, and to remove if possible the old landmarks of truth committed to God's people. He tries to make it appear as if the Lord contradicts Himself.

"It is when Satan appears as an angel of light, that he takes souls in his snare, deceiving them. Men who pretend to have been taught of God, will adopt fallacious theories, and in their teaching will so adorn these fallacies as to bring in Satanic delusions. Thus Satan will be introduced as an angel of light, and will have opportunity to present his pleasing fables.

"These false prophets will have to be met. They will make an effort to deceive many, by leading them to accept false theories. Many scriptures will be misapplied in such a way that deceptive theories will apparently be based upon the words that God has spoken. Precious truth will be appropriated to substantiate and establish error. These false prophets, who claim to be taught of God, will take beautiful scriptures that have been given to adorn the truth, and will use them as a robe of righteousness to cover false and dangerous theories. And even some of those who in times past the Lord has honored, will depart so far from the truth as to advocate misleading theories regarding many phases of truth, *including the sanctuary question*."—*Manuscript* 11, 1906. (Emphasis supplied.)

A few weeks later she added these words on the importance of a correct understanding of this truth:

"I know that the sanctuary question stands in righteousness and truth, just as we have held it for so many years. It is the enemy that leads minds off on sidetracks. He is pleased when those who know the truth become engrossed in collecting scriptures to pile around erroneous theories, which have no foundation in truth. The scriptures thus used are misapplied; they were not given to substantiate error, but to strengthen truth."—*Gospel Workers,* page 303.

With Eyes Fixed on the Sanctuary

At no time are we to lose sight of the important work being done in our behalf in the sanctuary in heaven. We are admonished:

"As a people, we should be earnest students of prophecy; we should not rest until we become intelligent in regard to the subject of the sanctuary, which is brought out in the visions of Daniel and John. This subject sheds great light on our present position and work, and gives us unmistakable proof that God has led us in our past experience. It explains our disappointment in 1844, showing us that the sanctuary to be cleansed was not the earth, as we had supposed, but that Christ then entered into the most holy apartment of the heavenly sanctuary, and is there performing the closing work of His priestly office, in fulfillment of the words of the angel to the prophet Daniel, 'Unto two thousand and three hundred days; then shall the sanctuary be cleansed.'

"Our faith in reference to the messages of the first, second, and third angels was correct. The great waymarks we have passed are immovable. Although the hosts of hell may try to tear them from their foundation, and triumph in the thought that they have succeeded, yet they do not succeed. These pillars of truth stand firm as the eternal hills, unmoved by all the efforts of men combined with those of Satan and his host. We can learn much, and should be constantly searching the Scriptures to see if these things are so. God's people are now to have their eyes fixed on the heavenly sanctuary, where the final ministration of our great High Priest in the work of the judgment is going forward,—where He is interceding for His people."—*Evangelism,* pages 222, 223.

This Little Book

Except for a few footnotes and the study questions which follow each chapter, the materials which follow are exclusively from the pen of Ellen G. White and consist primarily of chapters from *Patriarchs and Prophets* and *The Great Controversy*, with some bridging materials drawn together from various E. G. White published writings. In each case the source is given. As most readers will have at hand the E. G. White books, it has seemed unnecessary here, where brevity is desirable, to include portions of chapters not immediately relevant to the subject—Christ in His sanctuary.—The White Trustees.

Christ in the Sacrificial System *

The sin of our first parents brought guilt and sorrow upon the world, and had it not been for the goodness and mercy of God, would have plunged the race into hopeless despair.[1]

The fall of man filled all heaven with sorrow. The world that God had made was blighted with the curse of sin and inhabited by beings doomed to misery and death. There appeared no escape for those who had transgressed the law. . . .

But divine love had conceived a plan whereby man might be redeemed. The broken law of God demanded the life of the sinner. In all the universe there was but one who could, in behalf of man, satisfy its claims. Since the divine law is as sacred as God Himself, only one equal with God could make atonement for its transgression.[2]

To man the first intimation of redemption was communicated in the sentence pronounced upon Satan in the garden. The Lord declared, "I will put enmity between thee and the woman, and between thy seed and her seed; it shall bruise thy head, and thou shalt bruise his heel." Genesis 3:15. This sentence, uttered in the hearing of our first parents, was to them a promise. While it foretold war between man and Satan, it declared that the power of the great adversary would finally be broken. . . . Though they must suffer from the power of their mighty foe, they could look forward to final victory.[3]

---

*The statements comprising this chapter are drawn from *Patriarchs and Prophets* and other E. G. White published materials.

Heavenly angels more fully opened to our first parents the plan that had been devised for their salvation. Adam and his companion were assured that notwithstanding their great sin, they were not to be abandoned to the control of Satan. The Son of God had offered to atone, with His own life, for their transgression. A period of probation would be granted them, and through repentance, and faith in Christ, they might again become the children of God.

The Sacred Character of God's Law

The sacrifice demanded by their transgression, revealed to Adam and Eve the sacred character of the law of God; and they saw, as they had never seen before, the guilt of sin, and its dire results.[4]

The law of God existed before man was created. The angels were governed by it. Satan fell because he transgressed the principles of God's government. After Adam and Eve were created, God made known to them His law. It was not then written, but was rehearsed to them by Jehovah. . . .

After Adam's sin and fall, nothing was taken from the law of God. The principles of the Ten Commandments existed before the fall, and were of a character suited to the condition of a holy order of beings.[5]

The principles were more explicitly stated to man after the fall, and worded to meet the case of fallen intelligences. This was necessary in consequence of the minds of men being blinded by transgression.[6]

A system was then established requiring the sacrificing of beasts, to keep before fallen man that which the serpent made Eve disbelieve, that the penalty of disobedience is death. The transgression of God's law made it necessary for Christ to die a sacrifice, and thus make a way possible for man to escape the penalty, and yet the honor of God's law be preserved. The system of sacrifices was to teach man humility, in view of his fallen condition, and lead him to repentance, and to trust in God alone, through the promised Redeemer, for pardon for past transgression of His law.[7]

The very system of sacrifices was devised by Christ, and given to Adam as typifying a Saviour to come.[8]

Man Offers His First Sacrifice

To Adam, the offering of the first sacrifice was a most painful ceremony. His hand must be raised to take life, which only God could give. It was the first time he had ever witnessed death, and he knew that had he been obedient to God, there would have been no death of man or beast. As he slew the innocent victim, he trembled at the thought that his sin must shed the blood of the spotless Lamb of God. This scene gave him a deeper and more vivid sense of the greatness of his transgression, which nothing but the death of God's dear Son could expiate. And he marveled at the infinite goodness that would give such a ransom to save the guilty. A star of hope illumined the dark and terrible future and relieved it of its utter desolation.[9]

Adam was commanded to teach his descendants the fear of the Lord, and, by his example and humble obedience, teach them to highly regard the offerings which typified a Saviour to come. Adam carefully treasured what God had revealed to him, and handed it down by word of mouth to his children and children's children.[10]

At the cherubim-guarded gate of Paradise the glory of God was revealed, and hither came the first worshipers. Here their altars were reared, and their offerings presented.[11]

In the sacrificial offering on every altar was seen a Redeemer. With the cloud of incense arose from every contrite heart the prayer that God would accept their offerings as showing faith in the coming Saviour.[12]

The sacrificial system, committed to Adam, was . . . perverted by his descendants. Superstition, idolatry, cruelty, and licentiousness corrupted the simple and significant service that God had appointed. Through long intercourse with idolaters, the people of Israel had mingled many heathen customs with their worship; therefore the Lord gave them at Sinai definite instruction concerning the sacrificial service.[13]

---

1. *Patriarchs and Prophets,* page 61.
2. *Ibid.* p. 63.
3. *Ibid.*, pp. 65, 66.
4. *Ibid.*, p. 66.
5. *Spirit of Prophecy,* Vol. I, p. 261.
6. *Signs of the Times,* April 15, 1875.
7. *Spirit of Prophecy,* Vol. I, pp. 261, 262.
8. *Signs of the Times,* July 15, 1880.
9. *Patriarchs and Prophets,* page 68.
10. *Spirit of Prophecy,* Vol. I, page 59.
11. *Patriarchs and Prophets,* pages 83, 84.
12. *Review and Herald,* March 2, 1886.
13. *Patriarchs and Prophets,* page 364.

STUDY QUESTIONS

1. Why could only one equal with God make atonement for transgression of divine law? (19)
2. What meaning did the declaration of Genesis 3:15 have for Satan? For Adam and Eve? (19)
3. Why was a period of probation granted? (20)
4. What were the purposes of the system of sacrifices? (20, 21)
5. For what reasons was the first sacrifice by Adam a "painful ceremony"? (21)
6. Where did Adam and Eve set up their first altars? Is this significant? (21)

The Heavenly Sanctuary in Miniature

The command was communicated to Moses while in the mount with God, "Let them make Me a sanctuary; that I may dwell among them;" and full directions were given for the construction of the tabernacle. By their apostasy the Israelites forfeited the blessing of the divine Presence, and for the time rendered impossible the erection of a sanctuary for God among them. But after they were again taken into favor with Heaven, the great leader proceeded to execute the divine command.

Chosen men were especially endowed by God with skill and wisdom for the construction of the sacred building. God Himself gave to Moses the plan of that structure, with particular directions as to its size and form, the materials to be employed, and every article of furniture which it was to contain. The holy places made with hands were to be "figures of the true," "patterns of things in the heavens" (Hebrews 9:24, 23)—a miniature representation of the heavenly temple where Christ, our great High Priest, after offering His life as a sacrifice, was to minister in the sinner's behalf. God presented before Moses in the mount a view of the heavenly sanctuary, and commanded him to make all things according to the pattern shown him. All these directions were carefully recorded by Moses, who communicated them to the leaders of the people.

For the building of the sanctuary great and expensive preparations were necessary; a large amount of the most precious and costly material was required; yet the Lord accepted only freewill offerings. "Of every man that giveth it willingly with his heart ye shall take My offering" was the divine command repeated by Moses to the congregation. Devotion to God and a spirit of sacrifice were the first requisites in preparing a dwelling place for the Most High.

All the people responded with one accord. "They came, every one whose heart stirred him up, and every one whom his spirit made willing, and they brought the Lord's offering to the work of the tabernacle of the congregation, and for all His service, and for the holy garments. And they came, both men and women, as many as were willinghearted, and brought bracelets, and earrings, and rings, and tablets, all jewels of gold: and every man that offered, offered an offering of gold unto the Lord."

"And every man with whom was found blue, and purple, and scarlet, and fine linen, and goats' hair, and rams' skins dyed red, and sealskins, brought them. Everyone that did offer an offering of silver and brass brought the Lord's offering: and every man, with whom was found acacia wood for any work of the service, brought it.

"And all the women that were wisehearted did spin with their hands, and brought that which they had spun, the blue, and the purple, the scarlet, and the fine linen. And all the women whose heart stirred them up in wisdom spun the goats' hair.

"And the rulers brought the onyx stones, and the stones to be set, for the ephod, and for the breastplate; and the spice, and the oil; for the light, and for the anointing oil, and for the sweet incense." Exodus 35:23-28, R.V.

While the building of the sanctuary was in progress the people, old and young—men, women, and children—continued to bring their offerings, until those in charge of the work found that they had enough, and even more than could be used. And Moses caused to be proclaimed throughout the camp, "Let neither man nor woman make any more work for the offering of the sanctuary. So the people were restrained from bringing." The murmurings of the Israelites and the visitations of God's judgments because of their sins are recorded as a warning to after-generations. And their devotion, their zeal and liberality, are an example worthy of imitation. All who love the worship of God and prize the blessing of His sacred presence will manifest the same spirit of sacrifice in preparing a house where He may meet with them. They will desire to bring to the Lord an offering of the very best that they possess. A house built for God should not be left in debt, for He is thereby dishonored. An amount sufficient to accomplish the work should be freely given, that the workmen may be able to say, . . . "Bring no more offerings."

The Tabernacle and Its Construction

The tabernacle was so constructed that it could be taken apart and borne with the Israelites in all their journeyings. It was therefore small, being not more than fifty-five feet in length, and eighteen in breadth and height. Yet it was a magnificent structure. The wood employed for the building and its furniture was that of the acacia tree, which was less subject to decay than any other to be obtained at Sinai. The walls consisted of upright boards, set in silver sockets, and held firm by pillars and connecting bars; and all were overlaid with gold, giving to the building the appearance of solid gold. The roof was formed of four sets of curtains, the innermost of "fine twined linen, and blue, and purple, and scarlet: with cherubim of cunning work;" the other three respectively were of goats' hair, rams' skins dyed red, and sealskins, so arranged as to afford complete protection.

The building was divided into two apartments by a rich and beautiful curtain, or veil, suspended from gold-plated pillars; and a similar veil closed the entrance of the first apartment. These, like the inner covering, which formed the ceiling, were of the most gorgeous colors, blue, purple, and scarlet, beautifully arranged, while inwrought with threads of gold and silver were cherubim to represent the angelic host who are connected with the work of the heavenly sanctuary and who are ministering spirits to the people of God on earth.

The sacred tent was enclosed in an open space called the court, which was surrounded by hangings, or screens, of fine linen, suspended from pillars of brass. The entrance to this enclosure was at the eastern end. It was closed by curtains of costly material and beautiful workmanship, though inferior to those of the sanctuary. The hangings of the court being only about half as high as the walls of the tabernacle, the building could be plainly seen by the people without. In the court, and nearest the entrance, stood the brazen altar of burnt offering. Upon this altar were consumed all the sacrifices made by fire unto the Lord, and its horns were sprinkled with the atoning blood. Between the altar and the door of the tabernacle was the laver, which was also of brass, made from the mirrors that had been the freewill offering of the women of Israel. At the laver the priests were to wash their hands and their feet whenever they went into the sacred apartments, or approached the altar to offer a burnt offering unto the Lord.

In the first apartment, or holy place, were the table of showbread, the candlestick, or lampstand, and the altar of incense. The table of showbread stood on the north. With its ornamental crown, it was overlaid with pure gold. On this table the priests were each Sabbath to place twelve cakes, arranged in two piles, and sprinkled with frankincense. The loaves that were removed, being accounted holy, were to be eaten by the priests. On the south was the seven-branched candlestick, with its seven lamps. Its branches were ornamented with exquisitely wrought flowers, resembling lilies, and the whole was made from one solid piece of gold. There being no windows in the tabernacle, the lamps were never all extinguished at one time, but shed their light by day and by night. Just before the veil separating the holy place from the most holy and the immediate presence of God, stood the golden altar of incense. Upon this altar the priest was to burn incense every morning and evening; its horns were touched with the blood of the sin offering, and it was sprinkled with blood upon the great Day of Atonement. The fire upon this altar was kindled by God Himself and was sacredly cherished. Day and night the holy incense diffused its fragrance throughout the sacred apartments, and without, far around the tabernacle.

Beyond the inner veil was the holy of holies, where centered the symbolic service of atonement and intercession, and which formed the connecting link between heaven and earth. In this apartment was the ark, a chest of acacia wood, overlaid within and without with gold, and having a crown of gold about the top. It was made as a depository for the tables of stone, upon which God Himself had inscribed the Ten Commandments. Hence it was called the ark of God's testament, or the ark of the covenant, since the Ten Commandments were the basis of the covenant made between God and Israel.

The cover of the sacred chest was called the mercy seat. This was wrought of one solid piece of gold, and was surmounted by golden cherubim, one standing on each end. One wing of each angel was stretched forth on high, while the other was folded over the body (see Ezekiel 1:11) in token of reverence and humility. The position of the cherubim, with their faces turned toward each other, and looking reverently downward toward the ark, represented the reverence with which the heavenly host regard the law of God and their interest in the plan of redemption.

Above the mercy seat was the Shekinah, the manifestation of the divine Presence; and from between the cherubim, God made known His will. Divine messages were sometimes communicated to the high priest by a voice from the cloud. Sometimes a light fell upon the angel at the right, to signify approval or acceptance, or a shadow or cloud rested upon the one at the left to reveal disapproval or rejection.

The law of God, enshrined within the ark, was the great rule of righteousness and judgment. That law pronounced death upon the transgressor; but above the law was the mercy seat, upon which the presence of God was revealed, and from which, by virtue of the atonement, pardon was granted to the repentant sinner. Thus in the work of Christ for our redemption, symbolized by the sanctuary service, "mercy and truth are met together; righteousness and peace have kissed each other." Psalm 85:10.

No language can describe the glory of the scene presented within the sanctuary—the gold-plated walls reflecting the light from the golden candlestick, the brilliant hues of the richly embroidered curtains with their shining angels, the table, and the altar of incense, glittering with gold; beyond the second veil the sacred ark, with its mystic cherubim, and above it the holy Shekinah, the visible manifestation of Jehovah's presence; all but a dim reflection of the glories of the temple of God in heaven, the great center of the work for man's redemption.

A period of about half a year was occupied in the building of the tabernacle. When it was completed, Moses examined all the work of the builders, comparing it with the pattern shown him in the mount and the directions he had received from God. "As the Lord had commanded, even so had they done it: and Moses blessed them." With eager interest the multitudes of Israel crowded around to look upon the sacred structure. While they were contemplating the scene with reverent satisfaction, the pillar of cloud floated over the sanctuary and, descending, enveloped it. "And the glory of the Lord filled the tabernacle." There was a revealing of the divine majesty, and for a time even Moses could not enter. With deep emotion the people beheld the token that the work of their hands was accepted. There were no loud demonstrations of rejoicing. A solemn awe rested upon all. But the gladness of their hearts welled up in tears of joy, and they murmured low, earnest words of gratitude that God had condescended to abide with them.

The Priests and Their Attire

By divine direction the tribe of Levi was set apart for the service of the sanctuary. In the earliest times every man was the priest of his own household. In the days of Abraham the priesthood was regarded as the birthright of the eldest son. Now, instead of the first-born of all Israel, the Lord accepted the tribe of Levi for the work of the sanctuary. By this signal honor He manifested His approval of their fidelity, both in adhering to His service and in executing His judgments when Israel apostatized in the worship of the golden calf. The priesthood, however, was restricted to the family of Aaron. Aaron and his sons alone were permitted to minister before the Lord; the rest of the tribe were entrusted with the charge of the tabernacle and its furniture, and they were to attend upon the priests in their ministration, but they were not to sacrifice, to burn incense, or to see the holy things till they were covered.

In accordance with their office, a special dress was appointed for the priests. "Thou shalt make holy garments for Aaron thy brother, for glory and for beauty," was the divine direction to Moses. The robe of the common priest was of white linen, and woven in one piece. It extended nearly to the feet and was confined about the waist by a white linen girdle embroidered in blue, purple, and red. A linen turban, or miter, completed his outer costume. Moses at the burning bush was directed to put off his sandals, for the ground whereon he stood was holy. So the priests were not to enter the sanctuary with shoes upon their feet. Particles of dust cleaving to them would desecrate the holy place. They were to leave their shoes in the court before entering the sanctuary, and also to wash both their hands and their feet before ministering in the tabernacle or at the altar of burnt offering. Thus was constantly taught the lesson that all defilement must be put away from those who would approach into the presence of God.

The garments of the high priest were of costly material and beautiful workmanship, befitting his exalted station. In addition to the linen dress of the common priest, he wore a robe of blue, also woven in one piece. Around the skirt it was ornamented with golden bells, and pomegranates of blue, purple, and scarlet. Outside of this was the ephod, a shorter garment of gold, blue, purple, scarlet, and white. It was confined by a girdle of the same colors, beautifully wrought. The ephod was sleeveless, and on its gold-embroidered shoulder pieces were set two onyx stones, bearing the names of the twelve tribes of Israel.

Over the ephod was the breastplate, the most sacred of the priestly vestments. This was of the same material as the ephod. It was in the form of a square, measuring a span, and was suspended from the shoulders by a cord of blue from golden rings. The border was formed of a variety of precious stones, the same that form the twelve foundations of the City of God. Within the border were twelve stones set in gold, arranged in rows of four, and, like those in the shoulder pieces, engraved with the names of the tribes. The Lord's direction was, "Aaron shall bear the names of the children of Israel in the breastplate of judgment upon his heart, when he goeth in unto the holy place, for a memorial before the Lord continually." Exodus 28:29. So Christ, the great High Priest, pleading His blood before the Father in the sinner's behalf, bears upon His heart the name of every repentant, believing soul. Says the psalmist, "I am poor and needy; yet the Lord thinketh upon me." Psalm 40:17.

The Urim and Thummim

At the right and left of the breastplate were two large stones of great brilliancy. These were known as the Urim and Thummim. By them the will of God was made known through the high priest. When questions were brought for decision before the Lord, a halo of light encircling the precious stone at the right was a token of the divine consent or approval, while a cloud shadowing the stone at the left was an evidence of denial or disapprobation.

The miter of the high priest consisted of the white linen turban, having attached to it by a lace of blue, a gold plate bearing the inscription, "Holiness of Jehovah." Everything connected with the apparel and deportment of the priests was to be such as to impress the beholder with a sense of the holiness of God, the sacredness of His worship, and the purity required of those who came into His presence.

The Services of the Sanctuary*

Not only the sanctuary itself, but the ministration of the priests, was to "serve unto the example and shadow of heavenly things." Hebrews 8:5. Thus it was of great importance; and the Lord, through Moses, gave the most definite and explicit instruction concerning every point of this typical service. The ministration of the sanctuary consisted of two divisions, a daily and a yearly service. The daily service was performed at the altar of burnt offering in the court of the tabernacle and in the holy place; while the yearly service was in the most holy.

No mortal eye but that of the high priest was to look upon the inner apartment of the sanctuary. Only once a year could the priest enter there, and that after the most careful and solemn preparation. With trembling he went in before God, and the people in reverent silence awaited his return, their hearts uplifted in earnest prayer for the divine blessing. Before the mercy seat the high priest made the atonement for Israel; and in the cloud of glory, God met with him. His stay here beyond the accustomed time filled them with fear, lest because of their sins or his own he had been slain by the glory of the Lord.

The daily service consisted of the morning and evening burnt offering, the offering of sweet incense on the golden altar, and the special offerings for individual sins. And there were also offerings for sabbaths, new moons, and special feasts.

Every morning and evening a lamb of a year old was burned upon the altar, with its appropriate meat offering, thus symbolizing the daily consecration of the nation to Jehovah, and their constant dependence upon the atoning blood of Christ. God expressly directed that every offering presented for the service of the sanctuary should be "without blemish." Exodus 12:5. The priests were to examine all animals brought as a sacrifice, and

*Note: "After the completion of the tabernacle He [God] communicated with Moses from the cloud of glory above the mercy seat, and gave him full directions concerning the system of offerings and the forms of worship to be maintained in the sanctuary."—*Patriarchs and Prophets,* pages 364, 365.

were to reject every one in which a defect was discovered. Only an offering "without blemish" could be a symbol of His perfect purity who was to offer Himself as "a lamb without blemish and without spot." 1 Peter 1:19. The apostle Paul points to these sacrifices as an illustration of what the followers of Christ are to become. He says, "I beseech you therefore, brethren, by the mercies of God, that ye present your bodies a living sacrifice, holy, acceptable unto God, which is your reasonable service." Romans 12:1. We are to give ourselves to the service of God, and we should seek to make the offering as nearly perfect as possible. God will not be pleased with anything less than the best we can offer. Those who love Him with all the heart, will desire to give Him the best service of the life, and they will be constantly seeking to bring every power of their being into harmony with the laws that will promote their ability to do His will.

In the offering of incense the priest was brought more directly into the presence of God than in any other act of the daily ministration. As the inner veil of the sanctuary did not extend to the top of the building, the glory of God, which was manifested above the mercy seat, was partially visible from the first apartment. When the priest offered incense before the Lord, he looked toward the ark; and as the cloud of incense arose, the divine glory descended upon the mercy seat and filled the most holy place, and often so filled both apartments that the priest was obliged to retire to the door of the tabernacle. As in that typical service the priest looked by faith to the mercy seat which he could not see, so the people of God are now to direct their prayers to Christ, their great High Priest, who, unseen by human vision, is pleading in their behalf in the sanctuary above.

The incense, ascending with the prayers of Israel, represents the merits and intercession of Christ, His perfect righteousness, which through faith is imputed to His people, and which can alone make the worship of sinful beings acceptable to God. Before the veil of the most holy place was an altar of perpetual intercession, before the holy, an altar of continual atonement.

By blood and by incense God was to be approached—symbols pointing to the great Mediator, through whom sinners may approach Jehovah, and through whom alone mercy and salvation can be granted to the repentant, believing soul.

As the priests morning and evening entered the holy place at the time of incense, the daily sacrifice was ready to be offered upon the altar in the court without. This was a time of intense interest to the worshipers who assembled at the tabernacle. Before entering into the presence of God through the ministration of the priest, they were to engage in earnest searching of heart and confession of sin. They united in silent prayer, with their faces toward the holy place. Thus their petitions ascended with the cloud of incense, while faith laid hold upon the merits of the promised Saviour prefigured by the atoning sacrifice. The hours appointed for the morning and the evening sacrifice were regarded as sacred, and they came to be observed as the set time for worship throughout the Jewish nation. And when in later times the Jews were scattered as captives in distant lands, they still at the appointed hour turned their faces toward Jerusalem and offered up their petitions to the God of Israel. In this custom Christians have an example for morning and evening prayer. While God condemns a mere round of ceremonies, without the spirit of worship, He looks with great pleasure upon those who love Him, bowing morning and evening to seek pardon for sins committed and to present their requests for needed blessings.

The showbread was kept ever before the Lord as a perpetual offering. Thus it was a part of the daily sacrifice. It was called showbread, or "bread of the presence," because it was ever before the face of the Lord. It was an acknowledgment of man's dependence upon God for both temporal and spiritual food, and that it is received only through the mediation of Christ. God had fed Israel in the wilderness with bread from heaven, and they were still dependent upon His bounty, both for temporal food and spiritual blessings. Both the manna and the showbread pointed to Christ, the living Bread, who is ever in the presence of God for us. He Himself said, "I am the living Bread which came down from heaven." John 6:48-51. Frankincense was placed upon the loaves. When the bread was removed every Sabbath, to be replaced by fresh loaves, the frankincense was burned upon the altar as a memorial before God.

The most important part of the daily ministration was the service performed in behalf of individuals. The repentant sinner brought his offering to the door of the tabernacle, and, placing his hand upon the victim's head, confessed his sins, thus in figure transferring them from himself to the innocent sacrifice. By his own hand the animal was then slain, and the blood was carried by the priest into the holy place and sprinkled before the veil, behind which was the ark containing the law that the sinner had transgressed. By this ceremony the sin was, through the blood, transferred in figure to the sanctuary. In some cases the blood was not taken into the holy place; but the flesh was then to be eaten by the priest, as Moses directed the sons of Aaron, saying, "God hath given it you to bear the iniquity of the congregation." Leviticus 10:17.* Both ceremonies alike symbolized the transfer of the sin from the penitent to the sanctuary.

Such was the work that went on day by day throughout the year. The sins of Israel being thus transferred to the sanctuary, the holy places were defiled, and a special work became neces-

---

*NOTE: When a sin offering was presented for a priest or for the whole congregation, the blood was carried into the holy place and sprinkled before the veil and placed upon the horns of the golden altar. The fat was consumed upon the altar of burnt offering in the court, but the body of the victim was burned without the camp. See Leviticus 4:1-21.

When, however, the offering was for a ruler or for one of the people, the blood was not taken into the holy place, but the flesh was to be eaten by the priest, as the Lord directed Moses. See Leviticus 6:26; 4:22-35.

Thus, as the author describes elsewhere: "The sins of the people were transferred in figure to the officiating priest, who was a mediator for the people. The priest could not himself become an offering for sin, and make an atonement with his life, for he was also a sinner. Therefore, instead of suffering death himself, he killed a lamb without blemish; the penalty of sin was transferred to the innocent beast, which thus became his immediate substitute, and typified the perfect offering of Jesus Christ. Through the blood of this victim, man looked forward by faith to the blood of Christ which would atone for the sins of the world."—*Selected Messages,* Bk. 1, p. 230.

sary for the removal of the sins. God commanded that an atonement be made for each of the sacred apartments, as for the altar, to "cleanse it, and hallow it from the uncleanness of the children of Israel." Leviticus 16:19.

The Day of Atonement

Once a year, on the great Day of Atonement, the priest entered the most holy place for the cleansing of the sanctuary. The work there performed completed the yearly round of ministration.

On the Day of Atonement two kids of the goats were brought to the door of the tabernacle, and lots were cast upon them, "one lot for the Lord, and the other lot for the scapegoat." The goat upon which the first lot fell was to be slain as a sin offering for the people. And the priest was to bring his blood within the veil, and sprinkle it upon the mercy seat. "And he shall make an atonement for the holy place, because of the uncleanness of the children of Israel, and because of their transgressions in all their sins: and so shall he do for the tabernacle of the congregation, that remaineth among them in the midst of their uncleanness."

"And Aaron shall lay both his hands upon the head of the live goat, and confess over him all the iniquities of the children of Israel, and all their transgressions in all their sins, putting them upon the head of the goat, and shall send him away by the hand of a fit man into the wilderness: and the goat shall bear upon him all their iniquities unto a land not inhabited." Not until the goat had been thus sent away did the people regard themselves as freed from the burden of their sins. Every man was to afflict his soul while the work of atonement was going forward. All business was laid aside, and the whole congregation of Israel spent the day in solemn humiliation before God, with prayer, fasting, and deep searching of heart.

Important truths concerning the atonement were taught the people by this yearly service. In the sin offerings presented during the year, a substitute had been accepted in the sinner's stead; but the blood of the victim had not made full atonement for the sin. It had only provided a means by which the sin was transferred to the sanctuary. By the offering of blood, the sinner acknowledged the authority of the law, confessed the guilt of his transgression, and expressed his faith in Him who was to take away the sin of the world; but he was not entirely released from the condemnation of the law. On the Day of Atonement the high priest, having taken an offering for the congregation, went into the most holy place with the blood and sprinkled it upon the mercy seat, above the tables of the law. Thus the claims of the law, which demanded the life of the sinner, were satisfied. Then in his character of mediator the priest took the sins upon himself, and, leaving the sanctuary, he bore with him the burden of Israel's guilt. At the door of the tabernacle he laid his hands upon the head of the scapegoat and confessed over him "all the iniquities of the children of Israel, and all their transgressions in all their sins, putting them upon the head of the goat." And as the goat bearing these sins was sent away, they were, with him, regarded as forever separated from the people. Such was the service performed "unto the example and shadow of heavenly things." Hebrews 8:5.

A Figure of Things in the Heavens

As has been stated, the earthly sanctuary was built by Moses according to the pattern shown him in the mount. It was "a figure for the time then present, in which were offered both gifts and sacrifices;" its two holy places were "patterns of things in the heavens;" Christ, our great High Priest, is "a minister of the sanctuary, and of the true tabernacle, which the Lord pitched, and not man." Hebrews 9:9, 23; 8:2. As in vision the apostle John was granted a view of the temple of God in heaven, he beheld there "seven lamps of fire burning before the throne." He saw an angel "having a golden censer; and there was given unto him much incense, that he should offer it with the prayers of all saints upon the golden altar which was before the throne." Revelation 4:5; 8:3. Here the prophet was permitted to behold the first apartment of the sanctuary in heaven; and he saw there the "seven lamps of fire" and the "golden altar" represented by the golden candlestick and the altar of incense in the sanctuary on earth. Again, "the temple of God was opened" (Revelation 11:19), and he looked within the inner veil, upon the holy of holies. Here he beheld "the ark of His testament" (Revelation 11:19), represented by the sacred chest constructed by Moses to contain the law of God.

Moses made the earthly sanctuary, "according to the fashion that he had seen." Paul declares that "the tabernacle, and all the vessels of the ministry," when completed, were "the patterns of things in the heavens." Acts 7:44; Hebrews 9:21, 23. And John says that he saw the sanctuary in heaven. That sanctuary, in which Jesus ministers in our behalf, is the great original, of which the sanctuary built by Moses was a copy.

The heavenly temple, the abiding place of the King of kings, where "thousands ministered unto Him, and ten thousand times ten thousand stood before Him" (Daniel 7:10), that temple filled with the glory of the eternal throne, where seraphim, its shining guardians, veil their faces in adoration—no earthly structure could represent its vastness and its glory. Yet important truths concerning the heavenly sanctuary and the great work there carried forward for man's redemption were to be taught by the earthly sanctuary and its services.

After His ascension, our Saviour was to begin His work as our High Priest. Says Paul, "Christ is not entered into the holy places made with hands, which are the figures of the true; but into heaven itself, now to appear in the presence of God for us." Hebrews 9:24. As Christ's ministration was to consist of two great divisions, each occupying a period of time and having a distinctive place in the heavenly sanctuary, so the typical ministration consisted of two divisions, the daily and the yearly service, and to each a department of the tabernacle was devoted.

Christ in His Sanctuary

As Christ at His ascension appeared in the presence of God to plead His blood in behalf of penitent believers, so the priest in the daily ministration sprinkled the blood of the sacrifice in the holy place in the sinner's behalf.

The blood of Christ, while it was to release the repentant sinner from the condemnation of the law, was not to cancel the sin; it would stand on record in the sanctuary until the final atonement; so in the type the blood of the sin offering removed the sin from the penitent, but it rested in the sanctuary until the Day of Atonement.

Cleansed From the Record of Sin

In the great day of final award, the dead are to be "judged out of those things which were written in the books, according to their works." Revelation 20:12. Then by virtue of the atoning blood of Christ, the sins of all the truly penitent will be blotted from the books of heaven. Thus the sanctuary will be freed, or cleansed, from the record of sin. In the type, this great work of atonement, or blotting out of sins, was represented by the services of the Day of Atonement—the cleansing of the earthly sanctuary, which was accomplished by the removal, by virtue of the blood of the sin offering, of the sins by which it had been polluted.

As in the final atonement the sins of the truly penitent are to be blotted from the records of heaven, no more to be remembered or come into mind, so in the type they were borne away into the wilderness, forever separated from the congregation.

Since Satan is the originator of sin, the direct instigator of all the sins that caused the death of the Son of God, justice demands that Satan shall suffer the final punishment. Christ's work for the redemption of men and the purification of the universe from sin will be closed by the removal of sin from the heavenly sanctuary and the placing of these sins upon Satan, who will bear the final penalty. So in the typical service, the yearly round of ministration closed with the purification of the sanctuary, and the confessing of the sins on the head of the scapegoat.

Thus in the ministration of the tabernacle, and of the temple that afterward took its place, the people were taught each day the great truths relative to Christ's death and ministration, and once each year their minds were carried forward to the closing events of the great controversy between Christ and Satan, the final purification of the universe from sin and sinners.—*Patriarchs and Prophets*, pages 343-358.

STUDY QUESTIONS

1. What were the "first requisites" for preparing the sanctuary in the wilderness? (23)
2. What formed the basis for the plan for this sanctuary? How was it obtained? (23)
3. Is there significance to incense fragrance diffusing throughout the sanctuary and "far around the tabernacle"? (26, 27, 32, 33)
4. What was the manifestation of the divine Presence, and where did it appear? (27)
5. The law and the mercy seat were both in the most holy place. Why is this so? (27)
6. Why was the breastplate the most sacred of the priestly vestments? (30)
7. What *three* things were to be impressed upon Israel by the apparel and deportment of the priests? (30)
8. Why was the instruction on every part of the sanctuary services so explicit and definite? (30, 31)
9. How was the fact that the animal sacrifices were "without blemish" of double significance? (31, 32)
10. The offering of incense and blood was simultaneous. Why was this so? (32, 33)
11. In what two ways was sin transferred from the penitent to the sanctuary? (34)
12. When and how was the sanctuary cleansed from the sins of the people? (35, 36)
13. What objects did John see as in vision he viewed the first and second apartments of the heavenly sanctuary? What of its vastness and glory? (36)
14. How are the daily and yearly services of the sanctuary connected to each other? Apply this to Christ's ministry as our High Priest and the cleansing of the heavenly sanctuary from the record of sin. (37, 38)

The Gospel in Type and Antitype *

The long-cherished plan of David to erect a temple to the Lord, Solomon wisely carried out. For seven years Jerusalem was filled with busy workers engaged in leveling the chosen site, in building vast retaining walls, in laying broad foundations, —"great stones, costly stones, and hewed stones,"—in shaping the heavy timbers brought from the Lebanon forests, and in erecting the magnificent sanctuary. 1 Kings 5:17.

Simultaneously with the preparation of wood and stone, to which task many thousands were bending their energies, the manufacture of the furnishings for the temple was steadily progressing under the leadership of Hiram of Tyre, "a cunning man, endued with understanding, . . . skillful to work in gold, and in silver, in brass, in iron, in stone, and in timber, in purple, in blue, and in fine linen, and in crimson." 2 Chronicles 2:13, 14.

Perfect According to the Patterns

Thus as the building on Mount Moriah was noiselessly upreared with "stone made ready before it was brought thither: so that there was neither hammer nor ax nor any tool of iron heard in the house, while it was in building," the beautiful fittings were

*A chapter compiled from several E. G. White sources inserted here to provide a bridge between the typical sanctuary service on earth and the antitypical service in the heavenly sanctuary.

perfected according to the patterns committed by David to his son, "all the vessels that were for the house of God." 1 Kings 6:7; 2 Chronicles 4:19. These included the altar of incense, the table of shewbread, the candlestick and lamps, with the vessels and instruments connected with the ministrations of the priests in the holy place, all "of gold, and that perfect gold." 2 Chronicles 4:21. The brazen furniture,—the altar of burnt offering, the great laver supported by twelve oxen, the lavers of smaller size, with many other vessels,—"in the plain of Jordan did the king cast them, in the clay ground between Succoth and Zeredathah." 2 Chronicles 4:17. These furnishings were provided in abundance, that there should be no lack.

A Temple of Unrivaled Splendor

Of surpassing beauty and unrivaled splendor was the palatial building which Solomon and his associates erected for God and His worship. Garnished with precious stones, surrounded by spacious courts with magnificent approaches, and lined with carved cedar and burnished gold, the temple structure, with its broidered hangings and rich furnishings, was a fit emblem of the living church of God on earth, which through the ages has been building in accordance with the divine pattern, with materials that have been likened to "gold, silver, precious stones," "polished after the similitude of a palace." 1 Corinthians 3:12; Psalm 144:12.[1]

A most splendid sanctuary had been made, according to the pattern showed to Moses in the mount, and afterward presented by the Lord to David. In addition to the cherubim on the top of the ark, Solomon made two other angels of larger size, standing at each end of the ark, representing the heavenly angels guarding the law of God. It is impossible to describe the beauty and splendor of this sanctuary. Into this place the sacred ark was borne with solemn reverence by the priests, and set in its place beneath the wings of the two stately cherubim that stood upon the floor.

God Tokens His Acceptance

The sacred choir lifted their voices in praise to God, and the melody of their voices was accompanied by all kinds of musical instruments. And while the courts of the temple resounded with praise, the cloud of God's glory took possession of the house, as it had formerly filled the wilderness tabernacle. "And it came to pass, when the priests were come out of the holy place, that the cloud filled the house of the Lord, so that the priests could not stand to minister because of the cloud: for the glory of the Lord had filled the house of the Lord." 1 Kings 8:10, 11.

Like the earthly sanctuary built by Moses according to the pattern shown him in the mount, Solomon's temple, with all its services, was "a figure for the time then present, in which were offered both gifts and sacrifices;" its two holy places were "patterns of things in the heavens;" Christ, our great High Priest, is "a minister of the sanctuary, and of the true tabernacle, which the Lord pitched, and not man." [Hebrews 8:2.][2]

The whole system of types and symbols was a compacted prophecy of the gospel, a presentation in which were bound up the promises of redemption.[3]

The Antitype Lost Sight Of

The Lord Jesus was the foundation of the whole Jewish economy. Its imposing services were of divine appointment. They were designed to teach the people that at the time appointed One would come to whom those ceremonies pointed.[4]

As they departed from God, the Jews in a great degree lost sight of the teaching of the ritual service. That service had been instituted by Christ Himself. In every part it was a symbol of Him; and it had been full of vitality and spiritual beauty. But the Jews lost the spiritual life from their ceremonies, and clung to the dead forms. They trusted to the sacrifices and ordinances themselves, instead of resting upon Him to whom they pointed. In order to supply the place of that which they had lost, the priests and rabbis multiplied requirements of their own; and the more rigid they grew, the less of the love of God was manifested.[5]

The Temple Services Lost Their Significance

Christ was the foundation and life of the temple. Its services were typical of the sacrifice of the Son of God. The priesthood was established to represent the mediatorial character and work of Christ. The entire plan of sacrificial worship was a foreshadowing of the Saviour's death to redeem the world. There would be no efficacy in these offerings when the great event toward which they had pointed for ages was consummated.

Since the whole ritual economy was symbolical of Christ, it had no value apart from Him. When the Jews sealed their rejection of Christ by delivering Him to death, they rejected all that gave significance to the temple and its services. Its sacredness had departed. It was doomed to destruction. From that day sacrificial offerings and the service connected with them were meaningless. Like the offering of Cain, they did not express faith in the Saviour. In putting Christ to death, the Jews virtually destroyed their temple. When Christ was crucified, the inner veil of the temple was rent in twain from top to bottom, signifying that the great final sacrifice had been made, and that the system of sacrificial offerings was forever at an end.

"In three days I will raise it up." In the Saviour's death the powers of darkness seemed to prevail, and they exulted in their victory. But from the rent sepulcher of Joseph, Jesus came forth a conqueror. "Having spoiled principalities and powers, He made a show of them openly, triumphing over them." Colossians 2:15. By virtue of His death and resurrection He became the minister of the "true tabernacle, which the Lord pitched, and not man." Hebrews 8:2. Men reared the Jewish tabernacle; men builded the Jewish temple; but the sanctuary above, of which the earthly was a type, was built by no human architect. "Behold the Man whose name is The Branch; . . . He shall build the temple of the Lord; and He shall bear the glory, and shall sit and rule upon His throne; and He shall be a priest upon His throne." Zechariah 6:12, 13.

Eyes Turned to the True Sacrifice

The sacrificial service that had pointed to Christ passed away; but the eyes of men were turned to the true sacrifice for the sins of the world. The earthly priesthood ceased; but we look to Jesus, the minister of the new covenant, and "to the blood of sprinkling, that speaketh better things than that of Abel." "The way into the holiest of all was not yet made manifest, while as the first tabernacle was yet standing: . . . but Christ being come an high priest of good things to come, by a greater and more perfect tabernacle, not made with hands, . . . by His own blood He entered in once into the holy place, having obtained eternal redemption for us." Hebrews 12:24; 9:8-12.

"Wherefore He is able also to save them to the uttermost that come unto God by Him, seeing He ever liveth to make intercession for them." Hebrews 7:25. Though the ministration was to be removed from the earthly to the heavenly temple; though the sanctuary and our great high priest would be invisible to human sight, yet the disciples were to suffer no loss thereby. They would realize no break in their communion, and no diminution of power because of the Saviour's absence. While Jesus ministers in the sanctuary above, He is still by His Spirit the minister of the church on earth.[6]

Our High Priest, Our Advocate

"Christ is not entered into the holy places made with hands, which are the figures of the true; but into heaven itself, now to appear in the presence of God for us; nor yet that He should offer Himself often as the high priest entereth into the holy place every year with the blood of others; for then must He often have suffered since the foundation of the world: but now once in the end of the world hath He appeared to put away sin by the sacrifice of Himself." [Hebrews 9:24-26.] "This man, after He had offered one sacrifice for sins forever, sat down on the right hand of God." [Hebrews 10:12.] Christ entered in once into the holy place, having obtained eternal redemption for us. "Wherefore He is able also to save them to the uttermost that come unto God by Him, seeing He ever liveth to make intercession for them." [Hebrews 7:25.] He has qualified Himself to be not only man's representative, but his advocate, so that every soul, if he will, may say, I have a Friend at court, a High Priest who is touched with the feeling of my infirmities.[7]

The sanctuary in heaven is the very center of Christ's work in behalf of men. It concerns every soul living upon the earth. It opens to view the plan of redemption, bringing us down to the very close of time, and revealing the triumphant issue of the contest between righteousness and sin. It is of the utmost importance that all should thoroughly investigate these subjects, and be able to give to every one that asketh them a reason for the hope that is in them.[8]

---

1. *Prophets and Kings,* pages 35, 36.
2. *Review and Herald,* Nov. 9, 1905.
3. *The Acts of the Apostles,* page 14.
4. *Christ's Object Lessons,* page 34.
5. *The Desire of Ages,* page 29.
6. *Ibid.,* pp. 165, 166.
7. *Review and Herald,* June 12, 1900.
8. *Ibid.,* Nov. 9, 1905.

Christ in His Sanctuary

STUDY QUESTIONS

1. In what unique way was Solomon's temple constructed? (40)
2. Of what was the temple an emblem? (41)
3. How did God show His approval of the temple when it was completed? (42)
4. Around whom was the entire Jewish economy formed? (42)
5. When the Jews lost the spiritual life of their ceremonies, what did they do? (42, 43)
6. When and how did the temple lose its significance and sacredness? (43)
7. To what point and to whom was man then to look for a ministry significant to his salvation? (44)
8. Jesus is man's "representative" as well as his "advocate." What is the difference between these two functions? (44, 45)

The Judgment Message Stirs America

An upright, honest-hearted farmer, who had been led to doubt the divine authority of the Scriptures, yet who sincerely desired to know the truth, was the man specially chosen of God to lead out in the proclamation of Christ's second coming. Like many other reformers, William Miller had in early life battled with poverty and had thus learned the great lessons of energy and self-denial. The members of the family from which he sprang were characterized by an independent, liberty-loving spirit, by capability of endurance, and ardent patriotism—traits which were also prominent in his character. His father was a captain in the army of the Revolution, and to the sacrifices which he made in the struggles and sufferings of that stormy period may be traced the straitened circumstances of Miller's early life.

He had a sound physical constitution, and even in childhood gave evidence of more than ordinary intellectual strength. As he grew older, this became more marked. His mind was active and well developed, and he had a keen thirst for knowledge. Though he did not enjoy the advantages of a collegiate education, his love of study and a habit of careful thought and close criticism rendered him a man of sound judgment and comprehensive views. He possessed an irreproachable moral character and an enviable reputation, being generally esteemed for integrity, thrift, and benevolence. By dint of energy and application he early acquired a competence, though his habits of study were still maintained. He filled various civil and military offices with credit, and the avenues to wealth and honor seemed wide open to him.

His mother was a woman of sterling piety, and in childhood, he had been subject to religious impressions. In early manhood, however, he was thrown into the society of deists, whose influence was the stronger from the fact that they were mostly good citizens and men of humane and benevolent disposition. Living, as they did, in the midst of Christian institutions, their characters had been to some extent molded by their surroundings. For the excellencies which won them respect and confidence they were indebted to the Bible; and yet these good gifts were so perverted as to exert an influence against the word of God. By association with these men, Miller was led to adopt their sentiments. The current interpretations of Scripture presented difficulties which seemed to him insurmountable; yet his new belief, while setting aside the Bible, offered nothing better to take its place, and he remained far from satisfied. He continued to hold these views, however, for about twelve years. But at the age of thirty-four the Holy Spirit impressed his heart with a sense of his condition as a sinner. He found in his former belief no assurance of happiness beyond the grave. The future was dark and gloomy. . . .

In this state he continued for some months. "Suddenly," he says, "the character of a Saviour was vividly impressed upon my mind. It seemed that there might be a being so good and compassionate as to himself atone for our transgressions, and thereby save us from suffering the penalty of sin. I immediately felt how lovely such a being must be, and imagined that I could cast myself into the arms of, and trust in the mercy of, such a one. But the question arose, How can it be proved that such a being does exist? Aside from the Bible, I found that I could get no evidence of the existence of such a Saviour, or even of a future state. . . .

"I saw that the Bible did bring to view just such a Saviour as I needed; and I was perplexed to find how an uninspired book should develop principles so perfectly adapted to the wants of a fallen world. I was constrained to admit that the Scriptures must be a revelation from God. They became my delight; and in Jesus I found a friend. The Saviour became to me the chiefest among ten thousand; and the Scriptures, which before were dark and contradictory, now became the lamp to my feet and light to my path. My mind became settled and satisfied. I found the Lord God to be a Rock in the midst of the ocean of life. The Bible now became my chief study, and I can truly say, I searched it with great delight. I found the half was never told me. I wondered why I had not seen its beauty and glory before, and marveled that I could have ever rejected it. I found everything revealed that my heart could desire, and a remedy for every disease of the soul. I lost all taste for other reading, and applied my heart to get wisdom from God."—S. Bliss, *Memoirs of Wm. Miller,* pages 65-67.

Miller publicly professed his faith in the religion which he had despised. But his infidel associates were not slow to bring forward all those arguments which he himself had often urged against the divine authority of the Scriptures. He was not then prepared to answer them; but he reasoned that if the Bible is a revelation from God, it must be consistent with itself; and that as it was given for man's instruction, it must be adapted to his understanding. He determined to study the Scriptures for himself, and ascertain if every apparent contradiction could not be harmonized.

Endeavoring to lay aside all preconceived opinions, and dispensing with commentaries, he compared scripture with scripture by the aid of the marginal references and the concordance. He pursued his study in a regular and methodical manner; beginning with Genesis, and reading verse by verse, he proceeded no faster than the meaning of the several passages so unfolded as to leave him free from all embarrassment. When he found anything obscure, it was his custom to compare it with every other text which seemed to have any reference to the matter under consideration. Every word was permitted to have its proper bearing upon the subject of the text, and if his view of it harmonized with every collateral passage, it ceased to be a difficulty. Thus whenever he met with a passage hard to be understood he found an explanation in some other portion of the Scriptures. As he studied with earnest prayer for divine enlightenment, that which had before appeared dark to his understanding was made clear. He experienced the truth of the psalmist's words: "The entrance of Thy words giveth light; it giveth understanding unto the simple." Psalm 119:130.

The Study of the Prophecies

With intense interest he studied the books of Daniel and the Revelation, employing the same principles of interpretation as in the other scriptures, and found, to his great joy, that the prophetic symbols could be understood. He saw that the prophecies, so far as they had been fulfilled, had been fulfilled literally; that all the various figures, metaphors, parables, similitudes, etc., were either explained in their immediate connection, or the terms in which they were expressed were defined in other scriptures, and when thus explained, were to be literally understood. "I was thus satisfied," he says, "that the Bible is a system of revealed truths, so clearly and simply given that the wayfaring man, though a fool, need not err therein."—Bliss, page 70. Link after link of the chain of truth rewarded his efforts, as step by step he traced down the great lines of prophecy. Angels of heaven were guiding his mind and opening the Scriptures to his understanding.

Taking the manner in which the prophecies had been fulfilled in the past as a criterion by which to judge of the fulfillment of those which were still future, he became satisfied that the popular view of the spiritual reign of Christ—a temporal millennium before the end of the world—was not sustained by the word of God. This doctrine, pointing to a thousand years of righteousness and peace before the personal coming of the Lord, put far off the terrors of the day of God. But, pleasing though it may be, it is contrary to the teachings of Christ and His apostles, who declared that the wheat and the tares are to grow together until the harvest, the end of the world; that "evil men and seducers shall wax worse and worse;" that "in the last days perilous times shall come;" and that the kingdom of darkness shall continue until the advent of the Lord and shall be consumed with the spirit of His mouth and be destroyed with the brightness of His coming. Matthew 13:30, 38-41; 2 Timothy 3:13, 1; 2 Thessalonians 2:8.

The doctrine of the world's conversion and the spiritual reign of Christ was not held by the apostolic church. It was not generally accepted by Christians until about the beginning of the eighteenth century. Like every other error, its results were evil. It taught men to look far in the future for the coming of the Lord and prevented them from giving heed to the signs heralding His approach. It induced a feeling of confidence and security that was not well founded and led many to neglect the preparation necessary in order to meet their Lord.

Miller found the literal, personal coming of Christ to be plainly taught in the Scriptures. Says Paul: "The Lord Himself shall descend from heaven with a shout, with the voice of the Archangel, and with the trump of God." 1 Thessalonians 4:16. And the Saviour declares: "They shall *see* the Son of man coming in the clouds of heaven with power and great glory." "For as the lightning cometh out of the east, and shineth even unto the west; so shall also the coming of the Son of man be." Matthew 24:30, 27. He is to be accompanied by all the hosts of heaven. "The Son of man shall come in His glory, and all the holy angels with Him." Matthew 25:31. "And He shall send His angels with a great sound of a trumpet, and they shall gather together His elect." Matthew 24:31.

At His coming the righteous dead will be raised, and the righteous living will be changed. "We shall not all sleep," says Paul, "but we shall all be changed, in a moment, in the twinkling of an eye, at the last trump: for the trumpet shall sound, and the dead shall be raised incorruptible, and we shall be changed. For this corruptible must put on incorruption, and this mortal must put on immortality." 1 Corinthians 15:51-53. And in his letter to the Thessalonians, after describing the coming of the Lord, he says: "The dead in Christ shall rise first: then we which are alive and remain shall be caught up together with them in the clouds, to meet the Lord in the air: and so shall we ever be with the Lord." 1 Thessalonians 4:16, 17.

Not until the personal advent of Christ can His people receive the kingdom. The Saviour said: "When the Son of man shall come in His glory, and all the holy angels with Him, then shall He sit upon the throne of His glory: and before Him shall be gathered all nations: and He shall separate them one from another, as a shepherd divideth his sheep from the goats: and He shall set the sheep on His right hand, but the goats on the left. Then shall the King say unto them on His right hand, Come, ye blessed of My Father, inherit the kingdom prepared for you from the foundation of the world." Matthew 25:31-34. We have seen by the scriptures just given that when the Son of man comes, the dead are raised incorruptible and the living are changed. By this great change they are prepared to receive the kingdom; for Paul says: "Flesh and blood cannot inherit the kingdom of God; neither doth corruption inherit incorruption." 1 Corinthians 15:50. Man in his present state is mortal, corruptible; but the kingdom of God will be incorruptible, enduring forever. Therefore man in his present state cannot enter into the kingdom of God. But when Jesus comes, He confers immortality upon His people; and then He calls them to inherit the kingdom of which they have hitherto been only heirs.

These and other scriptures clearly proved to Miller's mind that the events which were generally expected to take place before the coming of Christ, such as the universal reign of peace and the setting up of the kingdom of God upon the earth, were to be subsequent to the second advent. Furthermore, all the signs of the times and the condition of the world corresponded to the prophetic description of the last days. He was forced to the conclusion, from the study of Scripture alone, that the period allotted for the continuance of the earth in its present state was about to close.

The Impact of Bible Chronology

"Another kind of evidence that vitally affected my mind," he says, "was the chronology of the Scriptures. . . . I found that predicted events, which had been fulfilled in the past, often occurred within a given time. The one hundred and twenty years to the flood (Genesis 6:3); the seven days that were to precede it, with forty days of predicted rain (Genesis 7:4); the four hundred years of the sojourn of Abraham's seed (Genesis 15:13); the three days of the butler's and baker's dreams (Genesis 40: 12-20); the seven years of Pharaoh's (Genesis 41:28-54); the forty years in the wilderness (Numbers 14:34); the three and a half years of famine (1 Kings 17:1) [see Luke 4:25;] . . . the seventy years' captivity (Jeremiah 25:11); Nebuchadnezzar's seven times (Daniel 4:13-16); and the seven weeks, threescore and two weeks, and the one week, making seventy weeks, determined upon the Jews (Daniel 9:24-27),—the events limited by these times were all once only a matter of prophecy, and were fulfilled in accordance with the predictions."—Bliss, pages 74, 75.

When, therefore, he found, in his study of the Bible, various chronological periods that, according to his understanding of them, extended to the second coming of Christ, he could not but regard them as the "times before appointed," which God had revealed unto His servants. "The secret things," says Moses, "belong unto the Lord our God: but those things which are revealed belong unto us and to our children forever;" and the Lord declares by the prophet Amos, that He "will do nothing, but He revealeth His secret unto His servants the prophets." Deuteronomy 29:29; Amos 3:7. The students of God's word may, then, confidently expect to find the most stupendous event to take place in human history clearly pointed out in the Scriptures of truth.

"As I was fully convinced," says Miller, "that all Scripture given by inspiration of God is profitable (2 Timothy 3:16); that it came not at any time by the will of man, but was written as holy men were moved by the Holy Ghost (2 Peter 1:21), and was written 'for our learning, that we through patience and comfort of the Scriptures might have hope' (Romans 15:4), I could but regard the chronological portions of the Bible as being as much a portion of the word of God, and as much entitled to our serious consideration, as any other portion of the Scriptures. I therefore felt that in endeavoring to comprehend what God had in His mercy seen fit to reveal to us, I had no right to pass over the prophetic periods."—Bliss, page 75.

The Prophecy of Daniel 8:14

The prophecy which seemed most clearly to reveal the *time* of the second advent was that of Daniel 8:14: "Unto two thousand and three hundred days; then shall the sanctuary be cleansed." Following his rule of making Scripture its own interpreter, Miller learned that a day in symbolic prophecy represents a year (Numbers 14:34; Ezekiel 4:6); he saw that the period of 2300 prophetic days, or literal years, would extend far beyond the close of the Jewish dispensation, hence it could not refer to the sanctuary of that dispensation. Miller accepted the generally received view that in the Christian age the earth is the sanctuary, and he therefore understood that the cleansing of the sanctuary foretold in Daniel 8:14 represented the purification of the earth by fire at the second coming of Christ. If, then, the correct starting point could be found for the 2300 days, he concluded that the time of the second advent could be readily ascertained. . . .

With a new and deeper earnestness, Miller continued the examination of the prophecies, whole nights as well as days being devoted to the study of what now appeared of such stupendous importance and all-absorbing interest. In the eighth chapter of Daniel he could find no clue to the starting point of the 2300 days; the angel Gabriel, though commanded to make Daniel understand the vision, gave him only a partial explanation. As the terrible persecution to befall the church was unfolded to the prophet's vision, physical strength gave way. He could endure no more, and the angel left him for a time. Daniel "fainted, and was sick certain days." "And I was astonished at the vision," he says, "but none understood it."

Yet God had bidden His messenger: "Make this man to understand the vision." That commission must be fulfilled. In obedience to it, the angel, some time afterward, returned to Daniel, saying: "I am now come forth to give thee skill and understanding;" "therefore understand the matter, and consider the vision." Daniel 8:27, 16; 9:22, 23, 25-27. There was one important point in the vision of chapter 8 which had been left unexplained, namely, that relating to time—the period of the 2300 days; therefore the angel, in resuming his explanation, dwells chiefly upon the subject of time:

"Seventy weeks are determined upon thy people and upon thy Holy City. . . . Know therefore and understand, that from the going forth of the commandment to restore and to build Jerusalem unto the Messiah the Prince shall be seven weeks, and threescore and two weeks: the street shall be built again, and the wall, even in troublous times. And after threescore and two weeks shall Messiah be cut off, but not for Himself. . . . And He shall confirm the covenant with many for one week: and in the midst of the week He shall cause the sacrifice and the oblation to cease."

The angel had been sent to Daniel for the express purpose of explaining to him the point which he had failed to understand in the vision of the eighth chapter, the statement relative to time —"unto two thousand and three hundred days; then shall the sanctuary be cleansed." After bidding Daniel "understand the matter, and consider the vision," the very first words of the angel are: "Seventy weeks are determined upon thy people and upon thy Holy City." The word here translated "determined" literally signifies "cut off." Seventy weeks, representing 490 years, are declared by the angel to be cut off, as specially pertaining to the Jews. But from what were they cut off? As the 2300 days was the only period of time mentioned in chapter 8, it must be the period from which the seventy weeks were cut off; the seventy weeks must therefore be a part of the 2300 days, and the two periods must begin together. The seventy weeks were declared by the angel to date from the going forth of the commandment to restore and build Jerusalem. If the date of this commandment could be found, then the starting point for the great period of the 2300 days would be ascertained.

In the seventh chapter of Ezra the decree is found. Verses 12-26. In its completest form it was issued by Artaxerxes, king of Persia, 457 B.C. But in Ezra 6:14 the house of the Lord at Jerusalem is said to have been built "according to the commandment ["decree," margin] of Cyrus, and Darius, and Artaxerxes king of Persia." These three kings, in originating, reaffirming, and completing the decree, brought it to the perfection required by the prophecy to mark the beginning of the 2300 years. Taking 457 B.C., the time when the decree was completed, as the date of the commandment, every specification of the prophecy concerning the seventy weeks was seen to have been fulfilled.

"From the going forth of the commandment to restore and to build Jerusalem unto the Messiah the Prince shall be seven weeks, and threescore and two weeks"—namely, sixty-nine weeks, or 483 years. The decree of Artaxerxes went into effect in the autumn of 457 B.C. From this date, 483 years extend to the autumn of A.D. 27.* At that time this prophecy was fulfilled. The word

*NOTE: According to Jewish reckoning the fifth month (Ab) of the seventh year of Artaxerxes' reign was from July 23 to August 21, 457 B.C. After Ezra's arrival in Jerusalem in the autumn of the year, the decree of the king went into effect. For the certainty of the date 457 B.C. being the seventh year of Artaxerxes, see S. H. Horn and L. H. Wood, *The Chronology of Ezra 7* (Washington, D.C.: Review and Herald Publishing Assn., 1953 and 1969); E. G. Kraeling, *The Brooklyn Museum Aramaic Papyri* (New Haven or London, 1953), pp. 191-193; *The Seventh-day Adventist Bible Commentary* (Washington, D.C.: Review and Herald Publishing Assn., 1954), Vol. 3, pp. 97-110.

"Messiah" signifies " the Anointed One." In the autumn of A.D. 27 Christ was baptized by John and received the anointing of the Spirit. The apostle Peter testifies that "God anointed Jesus of Nazareth with the Holy Ghost and with power." Acts 10:38. And the Saviour Himself declared: "The Spirit of the Lord is upon Me, because He hath anointed Me to preach the gospel to the poor." Luke 4:18. After His baptism He went into Galilee, "preaching the gospel of the kingdom of God, and saying, *The time* is fulfilled." Mark 1:14, 15.

"And He shall confirm the covenant with many for one week." The "week" here brought to view is the last one of the seventy; it is the last seven years of the period allotted especially to the Jews. During this time, extending from A.D. 27 to A.D. 34, Christ, at first in person and afterward by His disciples, extended the gospel invitation especially to the Jews. As the apostles went forth with the good tidings of the kingdom, the Saviour's direction was: "Go not into the way of the Gentiles, and into any city of the Samaritans enter ye not: but go rather to the lost sheep of the house of Israel." Matthew 10:5, 6.

"In the midst of the week He shall cause the sacrifice and the oblation to cease." In A.D. 31, three and a half years after His baptism, our Lord was crucified. With the great sacrifice offered upon Calvary, ended that system of offerings which for four thousand years had pointed forward to the Lamb of God. Type had met antitype, and all the sacrifices and oblations of the ceremonial system were there to cease.

The seventy weeks, or 490 years, especially allotted to the Jews, ended, as we have seen, in A.D. 34. At that time, through the action of the Jewish Sanhedrin, the nation sealed its rejection of the gospel by the martyrdom of Stephen and the persecution of the followers of Christ. Then the message of salvation, no longer restricted to the chosen people, was given to the world. The disciples, forced by persecution to flee from Jerusalem, "went everywhere preaching the word." "Philip went down to the city of Samaria, and preached Christ unto them." Peter, divinely guided, opened the gospel to the centurion of Caesarea, the God-fearing Cornelius; and the ardent Paul, won to the faith of Christ, was commissioned to carry the glad tidings "far hence unto the Gentiles." Acts 8:4, 5; 22:21.

Thus far every specification of the prophecies is strikingly fulfilled, and the beginning of the seventy weeks is fixed beyond question at 457 B.C., and their expiration in A.D. 34. From this data there is no difficulty in finding the termination of the 2300 days. The seventy weeks—490 days—having been cut off from the 2300, there were 1810 days remaining. After the end of 490 days, the 1810 days were still to be fulfilled. From A.D. 34, 1810 years extend to 1844. Consequently the 2300 days of Daniel 8:14 terminate in 1844. At the expiration of this great prophetic period, upon the testimony of the angel of God, "the sanctuary shall be cleansed." Thus the time of the cleansing of the sanctuary—which was almost universally believed to take place at the second advent—was definitely pointed out.

Miller and his associates at first believed that the 2300 days would terminate in the *spring* of 1844, whereas the prophecy points to the *autumn* of that year. The misapprehension of this point brought disappointment and perplexity to those who had fixed upon the earlier date as the time of the Lord's coming. But this did not in the least affect the strength of the argument showing that the 2300 days terminated in the year 1844, and that the great event represented by the cleansing of the sanctuary must then take place.

The Duty to Tell Others

Entering upon the study of the Scriptures as he had done, in order to prove that they were a revelation from God, Miller had not, at the outset, the slightest expectation of reaching the conclusion at which he had now arrived. . . . But the Scripture evidence was too clear and forcible to be set aside.

He had devoted two years to the study of the Bible, when, in 1818, he reached the solemn conviction that in about twenty-five years Christ would appear for the redemption of His people. "I need not speak," says Miller, "of the joy that filled my heart in view of the delightful prospect, nor of the ardent longings of my soul for a participation in the joys of the redeemed. The Bible was now to me a new book. It was indeed a feast of reason; all that was dark, mystical, or obscure to me in its teachings, had been dissipated from my mind before the clear light that now dawned from its sacred pages; and, oh, how bright and glorious the truth appeared! All the contradictions and inconsistencies I had before found in the word were gone; and although there were many portions of which I was not satisfied I had a full understanding, yet so much light had emanated from it to the illumination of my before darkened mind, that I felt a delight in studying the Scripture which I had not before supposed could be derived from its teachings."—Bliss, pages 76, 77.

"With the solemn conviction that such momentous events were predicted in the Scriptures to be fulfilled in so short a space of time, the question came home to me with mighty power regarding my duty to the world, in view of the evidence that had affected my own mind."—*Ibid.*, page 81. He could not but feel that it was his duty to impart to others the light which he had received. He expected to encounter opposition from the ungodly, but was confident that all Christians would rejoice in the hope of meeting the Saviour whom they professed to love. His only fear was that in their great joy at the prospect of glorious deliverance, so soon to be consummated, many would receive the doctrine without sufficiently examining the Scriptures in demonstration of its truth. He therefore hesitated to present it, lest he should be in error and be the means of misleading others. He was thus led to review the evidences in support of the conclusions at which he had arrived, and to consider carefully every difficulty which presented itself to his mind. He found that objections vanished before the light of God's words, as mist before the rays of the sun. Five years spent thus left him fully convinced of the correctness of his position.

And now the duty of making known to others what he believed to be so clearly taught in the Scriptures, urged itself with new force upon him. . . .

He began to present his views in private as he had opportunity, praying that some minister might feel their force and devote himself to their promulgation. But he could not banish the conviction that he had a personal duty to perform in giving the warning. The words were ever recurring to his mind: "Go and tell it to the world; their blood will I require at thy hand." For nine years he waited, the burden still pressing upon his soul, until in 1831 he for the first time publicly gave the reasons of his faith.

A Religious Awakening Begins

It was only at the solicitation of his brethren, in whose words he heard the call of God, that Miller consented to present his views in public. He was now fifty years of age, unaccustomed to public speaking, and burdened with a sense of unfitness for the work before him. But from the first his labors were blessed in a remarkable manner to the salvation of souls. His first lecture was followed by a religious awakening in which thirteen entire families, with the exception of two persons, were converted. He was immediately urged to speak in other places, and in nearly every place his labor resulted in a revival of the work of God. Sinners were converted, Christians were roused to greater consecration, and deists and infidels were led to acknowledge the truth of the Bible and the Christian religion. The testimony of those among whom he labored was: "A class of minds are reached by him not within the influence of other men."—*Ibid.*, page 138. His preaching was calculated to arouse the public mind to the great things of religion and to check the growing worldliness and sensuality of the age.

In nearly every town there were scores, in some, hundreds, converted as a result of his preaching. In many places Protestant churches of nearly all denominations were thrown open to him, and the invitations to labor usually came from the ministers of the several congregations. It was his invariable rule not to labor in any place to which he had not been invited, yet he soon found himself unable to comply with half the requests that poured in upon him.

Evidences of Divine Blessing

Many who did not accept his views as to the exact time of the second advent were convinced of the certainty and nearness of Christ's coming and their need of preparation. In some of the large cities his work produced a marked impression. Liquor dealers abandoned the traffic and turned their shops into meeting rooms; gambling dens were broken up; infidels, deists, Universalists, and even the most abandoned profligates were reformed, some of whom had not entered a house of worship for years. Prayer meetings were established by the various denominations, in different quarters, at almost every hour, businessmen assembling at midday for prayer and praise. There was no extravagant excitement, but an almost universal solemnity on the minds of the people. His work, like that of the early Reformers, tended rather to convince the understanding and arouse the conscience than merely to excite the emotions.

In 1833 Miller received a license to preach, from the Baptist Church, of which he was a member. A large number of the ministers of his denomination also approved his work, and it was with their formal sanction that he continued his labors. He traveled and preached unceasingly, though his personal labors were confined principally to the New England and Middle States. For several years his expenses were met wholly from his own private purse, and he never afterward received enough to meet the expense of travel to the places where he was invited. Thus his public labors, so far from being a pecuniary benefit, were a heavy tax upon his property, which gradually diminished during this period of his life. He was the father of a large family, but as they were all frugal and industrious, his farm sufficed for their maintenance as well as his own.

The Last of the Signs

In 1833, two years after Miller began to present in public the evidences of Christ's soon coming, the last of the signs appeared which were promised by the Saviour as tokens of His second advent. Said Jesus: "The stars shall fall from heaven." Matthew 24:29. And John in the Revelation declared, as he beheld in vision the scenes that should herald the day of God: "The stars of heaven fell unto the earth, even as a fig tree casteth her untimely figs, when she is shaken of a mighty wind." Revelation 6:13. This prophecy received a striking and impressive fulfillment in the great meteoric shower of November 13, 1833. That was the most extensive and wonderful display of falling stars which has ever been recorded; "the whole firmament, over all the United States, being then, for hours, in fiery commotion! No celestial phenomenon has ever occurred in this country, since its first settlement, which was viewed with such intense admiration by one class in the community, or with so much dread and alarm by another." "Its sublimity and awful beauty still linger in many minds. . . . Never did rain fall much thicker than the meteors fell toward the earth; east, west, north, and south, it was the same. In a word, the whole heavens seemed in motion. . . . The display, as described in Professor Silliman's *Journal,* was seen all over North America. . . . From two o'clock until broad daylight, the sky being perfectly serene and cloudless, an incessant play of dazzlingly brilliant luminosities was kept up in the whole heavens."—R. M. Devens, *American Progress; or, The Great Events of the Greatest Century,* ch. 28, pars. 1-5. . . .

In the New York *Journal of Commerce* of November 14, 1833, appeared a long article regarding this wonderful phenomenon, containing this statement: "No philosopher or scholar has told or recorded an event, I suppose, like that of yesterday morning. A prophet eighteen hundred years ago foretold it exactly, if we will be at the trouble of understand stars falling to mean falling stars, . . . in the only sense in which it is possible to be literally true."

Thus was displayed the last of those signs of His coming, concerning which Jesus bade His disciples: "When ye shall see all these things, *know* that it is near, even at the doors." Matthew 24:33. After these signs, John beheld, as the great event next impending, the heavens departing as a scroll, while the earth quaked, mountains and islands removed out of their places, and the wicked in terror sought to flee from the presence of the Son of man. Revelation 6:12-17.

Many who witnessed the falling of the stars, looked upon it as a herald of the coming judgment, "an awful type, a sure forerunner, a merciful sign, of that great and dreadful day." —"The Old Countryman," in Portland *Evening Advertiser,* Nov. 26, 1833. Thus the attention of the people was directed to the fulfillment of prophecy, and many were led to give heed to the warning of the second advent. . . .

The Bible and the Bible Only

William Miller possessed strong mental powers, disciplined by thought and study; and he added to these the wisdom of heaven by connecting himself with the Source of wisdom. He was a man of sterling worth, who could not but command respect and esteem wherever integrity of character and moral excellence were valued. Uniting true kindness of heart with Christian humility and the power of self-control, he was attentive and affable to all, ready to listen to the opinions of others and to weigh their arguments. Without passion or excitement he tested all theories and doctrines by the word of God, and his sound reasoning and thorough knowledge of the Scriptures enabled him to refute error and expose falsehood.

Yet he did not prosecute his work without bitter opposition. As with earlier Reformers, the truths which he presented were not received with favor by popular religious teachers. As these could not maintain their position by the Scriptures, they were driven to resort to the sayings and doctrines of men, to the traditions of the Fathers. But the word of God was the only testimony accepted by the preachers of the advent truth. "The Bible, and the Bible only," was their watchword. The lack of Scripture argument on the part of their opponents was supplied by ridicule and scoffing. Time, means, and talents were employed in maligning those whose only offense was that they looked with joy for the return of their Lord and were striving to live holy lives and to exhort others to prepare for His appearing. . . .

The instigator of all evil sought not only to counteract the effect of the advent message, but to destroy the messenger himself. Miller made a practical application of Scripture truth to the hearts of his hearers, reproving their sins and disturbing their self-satisfaction, and his plain and cutting words aroused their enmity. The opposition manifested by church members toward his message emboldened the baser classes to go to greater lengths; and enemies plotted to take his life as he should leave the place of meeting. But holy angels were in the throng, and one of these, in the form of a man, took the arm of this servant of the Lord and led him in safety from the angry mob. His work was not yet done, and Satan and his emissaries were disappointed in their purpose.

Despite all opposition, the interest in the advent movement had continued to increase. From scores and hundreds, the congregations had grown to as many thousands. Large accessions had been made to the various churches, but after a time the spirit of opposition was manifested even against these converts, and the churches began to take disciplinary steps with those who had embraced Miller's views. This action called forth a response from his pen, in an address to Christians of all denominations, urging that if his doctrines were false, he should be shown his error from the Scriptures.

"What have we believed," he said, "that we have not been commanded to believe by the word of God, which you yourselves allow is the rule, and only rule, of our faith and practice? What have we done that should call down such virulent denunciations against us from pulpit and press, and give you just cause to exclude us [Adventists] from your churches and fellowship?" "If we are wrong, pray show us wherein consists our wrong. Show us from the word of God that we are in error; we have had ridicule enough; that can never convince us that we are in the wrong; the word of God alone can change our views. Our conclusions have been formed deliberately and prayerfully, as we have seen the evidence in the Scriptures."—Bliss, pages 250, 252. . . .

Differing Responses

And why were the doctrine and preaching of Christ's second coming so unwelcome to the churches? While to the wicked the advent of the Lord brings woe and desolation, to the righteous it is fraught with joy and hope. This great truth had been the consolation of God's faithful ones through all the ages; why had it become, like its Author, "a stone of stumbling" and "a rock of offense" to His professed people? It was our Lord Himself who promised His disciples: "If I go and prepare a place for you, I will come again, and receive you unto Myself." John 14:3.

It was the compassionate Saviour, who, anticipating the loneliness and sorrow of His followers, commissioned angels to comfort them with the assurance that He would come again in person, even as He went into heaven. As the disciples stood gazing intently upward to catch the last glimpse of Him whom they loved, their attention was arrested by the words: "Ye men of Galilee, why stand ye gazing up into heaven? this same Jesus, which is taken up from you into heaven, shall so come in like manner as ye have seen Him go into heaven." Acts 1:11. Hope was kindled afresh by the angel's message. The disciples "returned to Jerusalem with great joy: and were continually in the temple, praising and blessing God." Luke 24:52, 53. They were not rejoicing because Jesus had been separated from them and they were left to struggle with the trials and temptations of the world, but because of the angel's assurance that He would come again.

The proclamation of Christ's coming should now be, as when

made by the angels to the shepherds of Bethlehem, good tidings of great joy. Those who really love the Saviour cannot but hail with gladness the announcement founded upon the word of God that He in whom their hopes of eternal life are centered is coming again, not to be insulted, despised, and rejected, as at His first advent, but in power and glory, to redeem His people. It is those who do not love the Saviour that desire Him to remain away, and there can be no more conclusive evidence that the churches have departed from God than the irritation and animosity excited by this Heaven-sent message.

Those who accepted the advent doctrine were roused to the necessity of repentance and humiliation before God. Many had long been halting between Christ and the world; now they felt that it was time to take a stand. . . . Christians were quickened to new spiritual life. They were made to feel that time was short, that what they had to do for their fellow men must be done quickly. Earth receded, eternity seemed to open before them, and the soul, with all that pertained to its immortal weal or woe, was felt to eclipse every temporal object. The Spirit of God rested upon them and gave power to their earnest appeals to their brethren, as well as to sinners, to prepare for the day of God. The silent testimony of their daily life was a constant rebuke to formal and unconsecrated church members. These did not wish to be disturbed in their pursuit of pleasure, their devotion to money-making, and their ambition for worldly honor. Hence the enmity and opposition excited against the advent faith and those who proclaimed it.

Investigation Discouraged

As the arguments from the prophetic periods were found to be impregnable, opposers endeavored to discourage investigation of the subject by teaching that the prophecies were sealed. . . .

Ministers and people declared that the prophecies of Daniel and the Revelation were incomprehensible mysteries. But Christ directed His disciples to the words of the prophet Daniel concerning events to take place in their time, and said: "Whoso readeth, let him *understand.*" Matthew 24:15. And the assertion that the Revelation is a mystery, not to be understood, is contradicted by the very title of the book: "The Revelation of Jesus Christ, which God gave unto Him, to show unto His servants things which must shortly come to pass. . . . *Blessed* is he that *readeth,* and they that *hear* the words of this prophecy, and *keep* those things which are written therein: for the time is at hand." Revelation 1:1-3. . . .

In view of the testimony of Inspiration, how dare men teach that the Revelation is a mystery beyond the reach of human understanding? It is a mystery revealed, a book opened. The study of the Revelation directs the mind to the prophecies of Daniel, and both present most important instruction, given of God to men, concerning events to take place at the close of this world's history.

To John were opened scenes of deep and thrilling interest in the experience of the church. He saw the position, dangers, conflicts, and final deliverance of the people of God. He records the closing messages which are to ripen the harvest of the earth, either as sheaves for the heavenly garner or as fagots for the fires of destruction. Subjects of vast importance were revealed to him, especially for the last church, that those who should turn from error to truth might be instructed concerning the perils and conflicts before them. None need be in darkness in regard to what is coming upon the earth.

Why, then, this widespread ignorance concerning an important part of Holy Writ? Why this general reluctance to investigate its teachings? It is the result of a studied effort of the prince of darkness to conceal from men that which reveals his deceptions. For this reason, Christ the Revelator, foreseeing the warfare that would be waged against the study of the Revelation, pronounced a blessing upon all who should read, hear, and observe the words of the prophecy.—*The Great Controversy,* pages 317-342.

Christ in His Sanctuary

STUDY QUESTIONS

1. What kind of man was William Miller? (47, 63)
2. What method of study did Miller use in his search of the Bible? (49, 50)
3. The doctrine of the world's conversion has led to what evil results? (51)
4. In what way did the text Daniel 8:14 become particularly significant? (54)
5. Miller was led to link the cleansing of the sanctuary with the second coming of Christ. What generally accepted view misled him? (54)
6. How and when did Jesus become "the Anointed One"? How and when did the "sacrifice and oblation" cease? (56, 57)
7. How were these events significant to the 2300-day prophecy of Daniel 8:14? (57, 58)
8. Miller spent seven years in earnest Bible study. How many were given to initial exploration? How many to careful review? (58-61)
9. For what reasons did Miller hesitate to begin preaching? (60)
10. In what way was Miller's preaching similar to that of the early Reformers? (61)
11. Why did Miller's preaching, like that of the Reformers, arouse opposition by "popular religious teachers"? How did these teachers make up for their lack of Scripture argument? (63, 64)
12. Why was the preaching of Christ's second coming so unwelcome to the churches? How did this same preaching affect those who accepted it? (65, 66)
13. Against what are those who read, hear, and observe the words of Revelation's prophecy protected? (67)

Daniel 8:14 and Steps in God's Mysterious Leadings

The work of God in the earth presents, from age to age, a striking similarity in every great reformation or religious movement. The principles of God's dealing with men are ever the same. The important movements of the present have their parallel in those of the past, and the experience of the church in former ages has lessons of great value for our own time.

No truth is more clearly taught in the Bible than that God by His Holy Spirit especially directs His servants on earth in the great movements for the carrying forward of the work of salvation. Men are instruments in the hand of God, employed by Him to accomplish His purposes of grace and mercy. Each has his part to act; to each is granted a measure of light, adapted to the necessities of his time, and sufficient to enable him to perform the work which God has given him to do. But no man, however honored of Heaven, has ever attained to a full understanding of the great plan of redemption, or even to a perfect appreciation of the divine purpose in the work for his own time. Men do not fully understand what God would accomplish by the work which He gives them to do; they do not comprehend, in all its bearings, the message which they utter in His name. . . .

Even the prophets who were favored with the special illumination of the Spirit did not fully comprehend the import of the revelations committed to them. The meaning was to be unfolded from age to age, as the people of God should need the instruction therein contained. . . .

Yet while it was not given to the prophets to understand fully the things revealed to them, they earnestly sought to obtain all the light which God had been pleased to make manifest. They "inquired and searched diligently," "searching what, or what manner of time the Spirit of Christ which was in them did signify." What a lesson to the people of God in the Christian age, for whose benefit these prophecies were given to His servants! "Unto whom it was revealed, that not unto themselves, but unto us they did minister." Witness those holy men of God as they "inquired and searched diligently" concerning revelations given them for generations that were yet unborn. Contrast their holy zeal with the listless unconcern with which the favored ones of later ages treat this gift of Heaven. What a rebuke to the ease-loving, world-loving indifference which is content to declare that the prophecies cannot be understood!

The Experience of the Apostles Provides an Object Lesson

Though the finite minds of men are inadequate to enter into the counsels of the Infinite One, or to understand fully the working out of His purposes, yet often it is because of some error or neglect on their own part that they so dimly comprehend the messages of Heaven. Not infrequently the minds of the people, and even of God's servants, are so blinded by human opinions, the traditions and false teaching of men, that they are able only partially to grasp the great things which He has revealed in His word. Thus it was with the disciples of Christ, even when the Saviour was with them in person. Their minds had become imbued with the popular conception of the Messiah as a temporal prince, who was to exalt Israel to the throne of the universal empire, and they could not understand the meaning of His words foretelling His sufferings and death.

Christ Himself had sent them forth with the message: "The time is fulfilled, and the kingdom of God is at hand: repent ye, and believe the gospel." Mark 1:15. That message was based on the prophecy of Daniel 9. The sixty-nine weeks were declared by the angel to extend to "the Messiah the Prince," and with high hopes and joyful anticipations the disciples looked forward to the establishment of Messiah's kingdom at Jerusalem to rule over the whole earth.

They preached the message which Christ had committed to them, though they themselves misapprehended its meaning. While their announcement was founded on Daniel 9:25, they did not see, in the next verse of the same chapter, that Messiah was to be cut off. From their very birth their hearts had been set upon the anticipated glory of an earthly empire, and this blinded their understanding alike to the specifications of the prophecy and to the words of Christ.

They performed their duty in presenting to the Jewish nation the invitation of mercy, and then, at the very time when they expected to see their Lord ascend the throne of David, they beheld Him seized as a malefactor, scourged, derided, and condemned, and lifted up on the cross of Calvary. What despair and anguish wrung the hearts of those disciples during the days while their Lord was sleeping in the tomb!

Christ had come at the exact time and in the manner foretold by prophecy. The testimony of Scripture had been fulfilled in every detail of His ministry. He had preached the message of salvation, and "His word was with power." The hearts of His hearers had witnessed that it was of Heaven. The word and the Spirit of God attested the divine commission of His Son. . . .

The announcement which had been made by the disciples in the name of the Lord was in every particular correct, and the events to which it pointed were even then taking place. "The time is fulfilled, the kingdom of God is at hand," had been their message. At the expiration of "the time"—the sixty-nine weeks of Daniel 9, which were to extend to the Messiah, "the Anointed One"—Christ had received the anointing of the Spirit after His baptism by John in Jordan. And the "kingdom of God" which they had declared to be at hand was established by the death of Christ. This kingdom was not, as they had been taught to believe, an earthly empire. Nor was it that future, immortal kingdom which shall be set up when "the kingdom and dominion, and the greatness of the kingdom under the whole heaven, shall be given to the people of the saints of the Most High;" that everlasting kingdom, in which "all dominions shall serve and obey Him." Daniel 7:27.

As used in the Bible, the expression "kingdom of God" is employed to designate both the kingdom of grace and the kingdom of glory. The kingdom of grace is brought to view by Paul in the Epistle to the Hebrews. After pointing to Christ, the compassionate intercessor who is "touched with the feeling of our infirmities," the apostle says: "Let us therefore come boldly unto *the throne of grace,* that we may obtain mercy, and find grace." Hebrews 4:15, 16. The throne of grace represents the kingdom of grace; for the existence of a throne implies the existence of a kingdom. In many of His parables Christ uses the expression "the kingdom of heaven" to designate the work of divine grace upon the hearts of men.

So the throne of glory represents the kingdom of glory; and this kingdom is referred to in the Saviour's words: "When the Son of man shall come in His glory, and all the holy angels with Him, then shall He sit upon the throne of His glory: and before Him shall be gathered all nations." Matthew 25:31, 32. This kingdom is yet future. It is not to be set up until the second advent of Christ.

The kingdom of grace was instituted immediately after the fall of man, when a plan was devised for the redemption of the guilty race. It then existed in the purpose and by the promise of God; and through faith, men could become its subjects. Yet it was not actually established until the death of Christ. Even after entering upon His earthly mission, the Saviour, wearied with the stubbornness and ingratitude of men, might have drawn back from the sacrifice of Calvary. In Gethsemane the cup of woe trembled in His hand. He might even then have wiped the bloodsweat from His brow and have left the guilty race to perish in their iniquity. Had He done this, there could have been no redemption for fallen men. But when the Saviour yielded up His life, and with His expiring breath cried out, "It is finished," then the fulfillment of the plan of redemption was assured. The promise of salvation made to the sinful pair in Eden was ratified. The kingdom of grace, which had before existed by the promise of God, was then established.

Thus the death of Christ—the very event which the disciples had looked upon as the final destruction of their hope—was that which made it forever sure. While it had brought them a cruel disappointment, it was the climax of proof that their belief had been correct. The event that had filled them with mourning and despair was that which opened the door of hope to every child of Adam, and in which centered the future life and eternal happiness of all God's faithful ones in all the ages. . . .

After His resurrection Jesus appeared to His disciples on the way to Emmaus, and, "beginning at Moses and all the prophets, He expounded unto them in all the Scriptures the things concerning Himself." Luke 24:27. The hearts of the disciples were stirred. Faith was kindled. They were "begotten again into a lively hope" even before Jesus revealed Himself to them. It was His purpose to enlighten their understanding and to fasten their faith upon the "sure word of prophecy." He wished the truth to take firm root in their minds, not merely because it was supported by His personal testimony, but because of the unquestionable evidence presented by the symbols and shadows of the typical law, and by the prophecies of the Old Testament. It was needful for the followers of Christ to have an intelligent faith, not only in their own behalf, but that they might carry the knowledge of Christ to the world. And as the very first step in imparting this knowledge, Jesus directed the disciples to "Moses and all the prophets." Such was the testimony given by the risen Saviour to the value and importance of the Old Testament Scriptures.

What a change was wrought in the hearts of the disciples as they looked once more on the loved countenance of their Master! Luke 24:32. In a more complete and perfect sense than ever before they had "found Him, of whom Moses in the law, and the prophets, did write." The uncertainty, the anguish, the despair, gave place to perfect assurance, to unclouded faith. What marvel that after His ascension they "were continually in the temple, praising and blessing God." The people, knowing only of the Saviour's ignominious death, looked to see in their faces the expression of sorrow, confusion, and defeat; but they saw there gladness and triumph. What a preparation these disciples had received for the work before them! . . .

The Lesson of 1844

The experience of the disciples who preached the "gospel of the kingdom" at the first advent of Christ, had its counterpart in the experience of those who proclaimed the message of His second advent. As the disciples went out preaching, "The time is fulfilled, the kingdom of God is at hand," so Miller and his associates proclaimed that the longest and last prophetic period brought to view in the Bible was about to expire, that the judgment was at hand, and the everlasting kingdom was to be ushered in. The preaching of the disciples in regard to time was based on the seventy weeks of Daniel 9. The message given by Miller and his associates announced the termination of the 2300 days of Daniel 8:14, of which the seventy weeks form a part. The preaching of each was based upon the fulfillment of a different portion of the same great prophetic period.

Like the first disciples, William Miller and his associates did not, themselves, fully comprehend the import of the message which they bore. Errors that had been long established in the church prevented them from arriving at a correct interpretation of an important point in the prophecy. Therefore, though they proclaimed the message which God had committed to them to be given to the world, yet through a misapprehension of its meaning they suffered disappointment.

In explaining Daniel 8:14, "Unto two thousand and three hundred days; then shall the sanctuary be cleansed," Miller, as has been stated, adopted the generally received view that the earth is the sanctuary, and he believed that the cleansing of the sanctuary represented the purification of the earth by fire at the coming of the Lord. When, therefore, he found that the close of the 2300 days was definitely foretold, he concluded that this revealed the time of the second advent. His error resulted from accepting the popular view as to what constitutes the sanctuary.

In the typical system, which was a shadow of the sacrifice and priesthood of Christ, the cleansing of the sanctuary was the last service performed by the high priest in the yearly round of ministration. It was the closing work of the atonement—a removal or putting away of sin from Israel. It prefigured the closing work in the ministration of our High Priest in heaven, in the removal or blotting out of the sins of His people, which are registered in the heavenly records. This service involves a work of investigation, a work of judgment; and it immediately precedes the coming of Christ in the clouds of heaven with power and great glory; for when He comes, every case has been decided. Says Jesus: "My reward is with Me, to give every man according as his work shall be." Revelation 22:12. It is this work of judgment, immediately preceding the second advent, that is announced in the first angel's message of Revelation 14:7: "Fear God, and give glory to Him; for the hour of His judgment is come."

Those who proclaimed this warning gave the right message at the right time. But as the early disciples declared, "The time is fulfilled, and the kingdom of God is at hand," based on the prophecy of Daniel 9, while they failed to perceive that the death of the Messiah was foretold in the same scripture, so Miller and his associates preached the message based on Daniel 8:14 and Revelation 14:7, and failed to see that there were still other messages brought to view in Revelation 14, which were also to be given before the advent of the Lord. As the disciples were mistaken in regard to the kingdom to be set up at the end of the seventy weeks, so Adventists were mistaken in regard to the event to take place at the expiration of the 2300 days. In both cases there was an acceptance of, or rather an adherence to, popular errors that blinded the mind to the truth. Both classes fulfilled the will of God in delivering the message which He desired to be given, and both, through their own misapprehension of their message, suffered disappointment.

Yet God accomplished His own beneficent purpose in permitting the warning of the judgment to be given just as it was. The great day was at hand, and in His providence the people were brought to the test of a definite time, in order to reveal to them what was in their hearts. The message was designed for the testing and purification of the church. They were to be led to see whether their affections were set upon this world or upon Christ and heaven. They professed to love the Saviour; now they were to prove their love. Were they ready to renounce their worldly hopes and ambitions, and welcome with joy the advent of their Lord? The message was designed to enable them to discern their true spiritual state; it was sent in mercy to arouse them to seek the Lord with repentance and humiliation.

The disappointment also, though the result of their own misapprehension of the message which they gave, was to be overruled for good. It would test the hearts of those who had professed to receive the warning. In the face of their disappointment would they rashly give up their experience and cast away their confidence in God's word? or would they, in prayer and humility, seek to discern where they had failed to comprehend the significance of the prophecy? How many had moved from fear, or from impulse and excitement? How many were half-hearted and unbelieving? Multitudes professed to love the appearing of the Lord. When called to endure the scoffs and reproach of the world, and the test of delay and disappointment, would they renounce the faith? Because they did not immediately understand the dealings of God with them, would they cast aside truths sustained by the clearest testimony of His word?

This test would reveal the strength of those who with real faith had obeyed what they believed to be the teaching of the word and the Spirit of God. It would teach them, as only such an experience could, the danger of accepting the theories and interpretations of men, instead of making the Bible its own interpreter. To the children of faith the perplexity and sorrow resulting from their error would work the needed correction. They would be led to a closer study of the prophetic word. They would be taught to examine more carefully the foundation of their faith, and to reject everything, however widely accepted by the Christian world, that was not founded upon the Scriptures of truth.

With these believers, as with the first disciples, that which in the hour of trial seemed dark to their understanding would afterward be made plain. When they should see the "end of the Lord" they would know that, notwithstanding the trial resulting from their errors, His purposes of love toward them had been steadily fulfilling. They would learn by a blessed experience that He is "very pitiful, and of tender mercy;" that all His paths "are mercy and truth unto such as keep His covenant and His testimonies."—*The Great Controversy*, pages 343-354.

STUDY QUESTIONS

1. What truth is very "clearly taught" in the Bible? (69)
2. Did God's servants, including the prophets, always fully understand their messages and work? (69)
3. Why is it that men often so dimly comprehend the messages of heaven? (70)
4. Although the message heralded by the disciples of Jesus was correct, what led them to misconceptions as to its intent and ultimately to their disappointment? (70-72)
5. What two meanings does the Biblical term "kingdom of God" have? When will these "kingdoms" be set up? (72)
6. What method did Jesus employ to lead the disciples to a correct understanding of His mission and their work? (73)
7. Name some parallels which may be drawn between the experience of the disciples and the Advent believers of 1844. (74-76)
8. What *two* vital lessons were learned by the disappointed Adventists of 1844? (77)

The End of the 2300 Days

A great religious awakening under the proclamation of Christ's soon coming is foretold in the prophecy of the first angel's message of Revelation 14. An angel is seen flying "in the midst of heaven, having the everlasting gospel to preach unto them that dwell on the earth, and to every nation, and kindred, and tongue, and people." "With a loud voice" he proclaims the message: "Fear God, and give glory to Him; for the hour of His judgment is come: and worship Him that made heaven, and earth, and the sea, and the fountains of waters." Verses 6, 7.

The fact that an angel is said to be the herald of this warning is significant. By the purity, the glory, and the power of the heavenly messenger, divine wisdom has been pleased to represent the exalted character of the work to be accomplished by the message and the power and glory that were to attend it. And the angel's flight "in the midst of heaven," the "loud voice" with which the warning is uttered, and its promulgation to all "that dwell on the earth,"—"to every nation, and kindred, and tongue, and people,"—give evidence of the rapidity and world-wide extent of the movement. . . .

Like the great Reformation of the sixteenth century, the advent movement appeared in different countries of Christendom at the same time. In both Europe and America men of faith and prayer were led to the study of the prophecies, and, tracing down the inspired record, they saw convincing evidence that the end of all things was at hand. In different lands there were isolated bodies of Christians who, solely by the study of the Scriptures, arrived at the belief that the Saviour's advent was near. . . .

To William Miller and his colaborers it was given to preach the warning in America. This country became the center of the great advent movement. It was here that the prophecy of the first angel's message had its most direct fulfillment. The writings of Miller and his associates were carried to distant lands. Wherever missionaries had penetrated in all the world, were sent the glad tidings of Christ's speedy return. Far and wide spread the message of the everlasting gospel: "Fear God, and give glory to Him; for the hour of His judgment is come." . . .

Waiting in Calm Expectancy

With unspeakable desire those who had received the message watched for the coming of their Saviour. The time when they expected to meet Him was at hand. They approached this hour with a calm solemnity. They rested in sweet communion with God, an earnest of the peace that was to be theirs in the bright hereafter. None who experienced this hope and trust can forget those precious hours of waiting.

For some weeks preceding the time, worldly business was for the most part laid aside. The sincere believers carefully examined every thought and emotion of their hearts as if upon their deathbeds and in a few hours to close their eyes upon earthly scenes. There was no making of "ascension robes"; but all felt the need of internal evidence that they were prepared to meet the Saviour; their white robes were purity of soul—characters cleansed from sin by the atoning blood of Christ.

Would that there were still with the professed people of God the same spirit of heart searching, the same earnest, determined faith. Had they continued thus to humble themselves before the Lord and press their petitions at the mercy seat they would be in possession of a far richer experience than they now have. There is too little prayer, too little real conviction of sin, and the lack of living faith leaves many destitute of the grace so richly provided by our Redeemer.

God designed to prove His people. His hand covered a mistake in the reckoning of the prophetic periods. Adventists did not discover the error, nor was it discovered by the most learned of their opponents. The latter said: "Your reckoning of the prophetic periods is correct. Some great event is about to take place; but it is not what Mr. Miller predicts; it is the conversion of the world, and not the second advent of Christ."

The time of expectation passed, and Christ did not appear for the deliverance of His people. Those who with sincere faith and love had looked for their Saviour, experienced a bitter disappointment. Yet the purposes of God were being accomplished; He was testing the hearts of those who professed to be waiting for His appearing. There were among them many who had been actuated by no higher motive than fear. Their profession of faith had not affected their hearts or their lives. When the expected event failed to take place, these persons declared that they were not disappointed; they had never believed that Christ would come. They were among the first to ridicule the sorrow of the true believers.

But Jesus and all the heavenly host looked with love and sympathy upon the tried and faithful yet disappointed ones. Could the veil separating the visible from the invisible world have been swept back, angels would have been seen drawing near to these steadfast souls and shielding them from the shafts of Satan.—*The Great Controversy,* pages 355-374.

The Scriptures Reexamined

When the time passed at which the Lord's coming was first expected,—in the spring of 1844,—those who had looked in faith for His appearing were for a season involved in doubt and uncertainty. While the world regarded them as having been utterly defeated and proved to have been cherishing a delusion, their source of consolation was still the word of God. Many continued to search the Scriptures, examining anew the evidences of their faith and carefully studying the prophecies to obtain further light. The Bible testimony in support of their position seemed clear and conclusive. Signs which could not be mistaken pointed to the coming of Christ as near. The special blessing of the Lord, both in the conversion of sinners and the revival of spiritual life among Christians, had testified that the message was of Heaven. And though the believers could not explain their disappointment, they felt assured that God had led them in their past experience.

Interwoven with prophecies which they had regarded as applying to the time of the second advent was instruction specially adapted to their state of uncertainty and suspense, and encouraging them to wait patiently in the faith that what was now dark to their understanding would in due time be made plain. . . .

In the summer of 1844, midway between the time when it had been first thought that the 2300 days would end, and the autumn of the same year, to which it was afterward found that they extended, the message was proclaimed in the very words of Scripture: "Behold, the Bridegroom cometh!"

That which led to this movement was the discovery that the decree of Artaxerxes for the restoration of Jerusalem, which formed the starting point for the period of the 2300 days, went into effect in the autumn of the year 457 B.C., and not at the beginning of the year, as had been formerly believed. Reckoning from the autumn of 457, the 2300 years terminate in the autumn of 1844.

Types in the Sanctuary Service

Arguments drawn from the Old Testament types also pointed to the autumn as the time when the event represented by the "cleansing of the sanctury" must take place. This was made very clear as attention was given to the manner in which the types relating to the first advent of Christ had been fulfilled.

The slaying of the Passover lamb was a shadow of the death

of Christ. Says Paul: "Christ our Passover is sacrificed for us." 1 Corinthians 5:7. The sheaf of first fruits, which at the time of the Passover was waved before the Lord, was typical of the resurrection of Christ. . . .

These types were fulfilled, not only as to the event, but as to the time. On the fourteenth day of the first Jewish month, the very day and month on which for fifteen long centuries the Passover lamb had been slain, Christ, having eaten the Passover with His disciples, instituted that feast which was to commemorate His own death as "the Lamb of God, which taketh away the sin of the world." That same night He was taken by wicked hands to be crucified and slain. And as the antitype of the wave sheaf our Lord was raised from the dead on the third day, "the first fruits of them that slept," a sample of all the resurrected just, whose "vile body" shall be changed, and "fashioned like unto His glorious body." Verse 20; Philippians 3:21.

In like manner the types which relate to the second advent must be fulfilled at the time pointed out in the symbolic service. Under the Mosaic system the cleansing of the sanctuary, or the great Day of Atonement, occurred on the tenth day of the seventh Jewish month (Leviticus 16:29-34), when the high priest, having made an atonement for all Israel, and thus removed their sins from the sanctuary, came forth and blessed the people. So it was believed that Christ, our great High Priest, would appear to purify the earth by the destruction of sin and sinners, and to bless His waiting people with immortality. The tenth day of the seventh month, the great Day of Atonement, the time of the cleansing of the sanctuary, which in the year 1844 fell upon the twenty-second of October, was regarded as the time of the Lord's coming. This was in harmony with the proofs already presented that the 2300 days would terminate in the autumn, and the conclusion seemed irresistible. . . .

Carefully and solemnly those who received the message came up to the time when they hoped to meet their Lord. Every morning they felt that it was their first duty to secure the evidence of their acceptance with God. Their hearts were closely united, and they prayed much with and for one another. They often met together in secluded places to commune with God, and the voice of intercession ascended to heaven from the fields and groves. The assurance of the Saviour's approval was more necessary to them than their daily food; and if a cloud darkened their minds, they did not rest until it was swept away. As they felt the witness of pardoning grace, they longed to behold Him whom their souls loved.

Disappointed, but Faith in God's Word Unshaken

But again they were destined to disappointment. The time of expectation passed, and their Saviour did not appear. With unwavering confidence they had looked forward to His coming, and now they felt as did Mary when, coming to the Saviour's tomb and finding it empty, she exclaimed with weeping: "They have taken away my Lord, and I know not where they have laid Him." John 20:13. . . .

The world had been looking on, expecting that if the time passed and Christ did not appear, the whole system of Adventism would be given up. But while many, under strong temptation, yielded their faith, there were some who stood firm. The fruits of the advent movement, the spirit of humility and heart searching, of renouncing of the world and reformation of life, which had attended the work, testified that it was of God. They dared not deny that the power of the Holy Spirit had witnessed to the preaching of the second advent, and they could detect no error in their reckoning of the prophetic periods. The ablest of their opponents had not succeeded in overthrowing their system of prophetic interpretation. They could not consent, without Bible evidence, to renounce positions which had been reached through earnest, prayerful study of the Scriptures, by minds enlightened by the Spirit of God and hearts burning with its living power; positions which had withstood the most searching criticisms and the most bitter opposition of popular religious teachers and worldly-wise men, and which had stood firm against the combined forces of learning and eloquence, and the taunts and revilings alike of the honorable and the base.

True, there had been a failure as to the expected event, but even this could not shake their faith in the word of God. . . .

God did not forsake His people; His Spirit still abode with those who did not rashly deny the light which they had received, and denounce the advent movement. In the Epistle to the Hebrews are words of encouragement and warning for the tried, waiting ones at this crisis: "Cast not away therefore your confidence, which hath great recompense of reward. For ye have need of patience, that, after ye have done the will of God, ye might receive the promise. For yet a little while, and He that shall come will come, and will not tarry. Now the just shall live by faith: but if any man draw back, My soul shall have no pleasure in him. But we are not of them who draw back unto perdition; but of them that believe to the saving of the soul." Hebrews 10:35-39.

That this admonition is addressed to the church in the last days is evident from the words pointing to the nearness of the Lord's coming: "For yet a little while, and He that shall come will come and will not tarry." And it is plainly implied that there would be a seeming delay and that the Lord would appear to tarry. The instruction here given is especially adapted to the experience of Adventists at this time. The people here addressed were in danger of making shipwreck of faith. They had done the will of God in following the guidance of His Spirit and His word; yet they could not understand His purpose in their past experience, nor could they discern the pathway before them, and they were tempted to doubt whether God had indeed been leading them. At this time the words were applicable: "Now the just shall live by faith."

As the bright light of the "midnight cry" had shone upon their pathway, and they had seen the prophecies unsealed and the rapidly fulfilling signs telling that the coming of Christ was near, they had walked, as it were, by sight. But now, bowed down by disappointed hopes, they could stand only by faith in God and in His word. The scoffing world were saying: "You have been deceived. Give up your faith, and say that the advent movement was of Satan." But God's word declared: "If any man draw back, My soul shall have no pleasure in him."

To renounce their faith now, and deny the power of the Holy Spirit which had attended the message, would be drawing back toward perdition. They were encouraged to steadfastness by the words of Paul: "Cast not away therefore your confidence;" "ye have need of patience," "for yet a little while, and He that shall come will come, and will not tarry." Their only safe course was to cherish the light which they had already received of God, hold fast to His promises, and continue to search the Scriptures, and patiently wait and watch to receive further light.—*The Great Controversy,* pages 391-408.

STUDY QUESTIONS

1. How is the "exalted character" of the message of the first angel of Revelation 14 represented? In what *three* ways are the rapidity and worldwide extent of the movement indicated? (79)
2. How widely was the warning message given? (79, 80)
3. What "robes" did the waiting Adventists prepare for Christ's second coming? (80)
4. What was the "source of consolation" for the Adventists after their first disappointment in the spring of 1844? (81, 82)
5. What was the Scripture message proclaimed during the summer of 1844? (82)
6. How did a study of types and antitypes lead to the establishment of the important date of October 22, 1844? (82, 83)
7. Name some of the things the Adventists did to prepare for the expected coming of Christ. (83, 84)
8. The fruits of the advent movement "testified it was of God." What were those fruits? (84)
9. What Scripture admonition is addressed to the church in the last days? (86)

The Glorious Temple in Heaven

The scripture which above all others had been both the foundation and the central pillar of the advent faith was the declaration: "Unto two thousand and three hundred days; then shall the sanctuary be cleansed." Daniel 8:14. These had been familiar words to all believers in the Lord's soon coming. By the lips of thousands was this prophecy repeated as the watchword of their faith. All felt that upon the events therein foretold depended their brightest expectations and most cherished hopes. These prophetic days had been shown to terminate in the autumn of 1844. In common with the rest of the Christian world, Adventists then held that the earth, or some portion of it, was the sanctuary. They understood that the cleansing of the sanctuary was the purification of the earth by the fires of the last great day, and that this would take place at the second advent. Hence the conclusion that Christ would return to the earth in 1844.

But the appointed time had passed, and the Lord had not appeared. The believers knew that God's word could not fail; their interpretation of the prophecy must be at fault; but where was the mistake? Many rashly cut the knot of difficulty by denying that the 2300 days ended in 1844. No reason could be given for this except that Christ had not come at the time they expected Him. They argued that if the prophetic days had ended in 1844, Christ would then have returned to cleanse the sanctuary by the purification of the earth by fire; and that since He had not come, the days could not have ended.

Integrity of the Prophetic Periods

To accept this conclusion was to renounce the former reckoning of the prophetic periods. The 2300 days had been found to begin when the commandment of Artaxerxes for the restoration and building of Jerusalem went into effect, in the autumn of 457 B.C. Taking this as the starting point, there was perfect harmony in the application of all the events foretold in the explanation of that period in Daniel 9:25-27. Sixty-nine weeks, the first 483 of the 2300 years, were to reach to the Messiah, the Anointed One; and Christ's baptism and anointing by the Holy Spirit, A.D. 27, exactly fulfilled the specification. In the midst of the seventieth week, Messiah was to be cut off. Three and a half years after His baptism, Christ was crucified, in the spring of A.D. 31. The seventy weeks, or 490 years, were to pertain especially to the Jews. At the expiration of this period the nation sealed its rejection of Christ by the persecution of His disciples, and the apostles turned to the Gentiles, A.D. 34. The first 490 years of the 2300 having then ended, 1810 years would remain. From A.D. 34, 1810 years extend to 1844. "Then," said the angel, "shall the sanctuary be cleansed." All the preceding specifications of the prophecy had been unquestionably fulfilled at the time appointed.

With this reckoning, all was clear and harmonious, except that it was not seen that any event answering to the cleansing of the sanctuary had taken place in 1844. To deny that the days ended at that time was to involve the whole question in confusion, and to renounce positions which had been established by unmistakable fulfillments of prophecy.

But God had led His people in the great advent movement; His power and glory had attended the work, and He would not permit it to end in darkness and disappointment, to be reproached as a false and fanatical excitement. He would not leave His word involved in doubt and uncertainty. Though many abandoned their former reckoning of the prophetic periods and denied the correctness of the movement based thereon, others were unwilling to renounce points of faith and experience that were sustained by the Scriptures and by the witness of the Spirit of God. They believed that they had adopted sound principles of interpretation in their study of the prophecies, and that it was their duty to hold fast the truths already gained, and to continue the same course of Biblical research. With earnest prayer they reviewed their position and studied the Scriptures to discover their mistake. As they could see no error in their reckoning of the prophetic periods, they were led to examine more closely the subject of the sanctuary.

The Sanctuary of the Old Covenant

In their investigation they learned that there is no Scripture evidence sustaining the popular view that the earth is the sanctuary; but they found in the Bible a full explanation of the subject of the sanctuary, its nature, location, and services; the testimony of the sacred writers being so clear and ample as to place the matter beyond all question. The apostle Paul, in the Epistle to the Hebrews, says: "Then verily the first covenant had also ordinances of divine service, and a worldly sanctuary. For there was a tabernacle made; the first, wherein was the candlestick, and the table, and the shewbread; which is called the sanctuary. And after the second veil, the tabernacle which is called the holiest of all; which had the golden censer, and the ark of the covenant overlaid round about with gold, wherein was the golden pot that had manna, and Aaron's rod that budded, and the tables of the covenant; and over it the cherubims of glory shadowing the mercy seat." Hebrews 9:1-5.

The sanctuary to which Paul here refers was the tabernacle built by Moses at the command of God as the earthly dwelling place of the Most High. "Let them make Me a sanctuary; that I may dwell among them" (Exodus 25:8), was the direction given to Moses while in the mount with God. The Israelites were journeying through the wilderness, and the tabernacle was so constructed that it could be removed from place to place; yet it was a structure of great magnificence. . . .

After the settlement of the Hebrews in Canaan, the tabernacle was replaced by the temple of Solomon, which, though a permanent structure and upon a larger scale, observed the same proportions, and was similarly furnished. In this form the sanctuary existed—except while it lay in ruins in Daniel's time—until its destruction by the Romans, in A.D. 70.

This is the only sanctuary that ever existed on the earth, of which the Bible gives any information. This was declared by Paul to be the sanctuary of the first covenant. But has the new covenant no sanctuary?

The New-covenant Sanctuary in the Heavens

Turning again to the book of Hebrews, the seekers for truth found that the existence of a second, or new-covenant sanctuary, was implied in the words of Paul already quoted: "Then verily the first covenant had *also* ordinances of divine service, and a worldly sanctuary." And the use of the word "also" intimates that Paul has before made mention of this sanctuary. Turning back to the beginning of the previous chapter, they read: "Now of the things which we have spoken this is the sum: We have such an High Priest, who is set on the right hand of the throne of the Majesty in the heavens; a Minister of the sanctuary, and of the true tabernacle, which the Lord pitched, and not man." Hebrews 8:1, 2.

Here is revealed the sanctuary of the new covenant. The sanctuary of the first covenant was pitched by man, built by Moses; this is pitched by the Lord, not by man. In that sanctuary the earthly priests performed their service; in this, Christ, our great High Priest, ministers at God's right hand. One sanctuary was on earth, the other is in heaven.

Further, the tabernacle built by Moses was made after a pattern. The Lord directed him: "According to all that I show thee, after the pattern of the tabernacle, and the pattern of all the instruments thereof, even so shall ye make it." And again the charge was given, "Look that thou make them after their pattern, which was showed thee in the mount." Exodus 25:9, 40. And Paul says that the first tabernacle "was a figure for the time then present, in which were offered both gifts and sacrifices;" that its holy places were "patterns of things in the heavens;" that the priests who offered gifts according to the law served "unto the example and shadow of heavenly things," and that "Christ is not entered into the holy places made with hands, which are the figures of the true; but into heaven itself, now to appear in the presence of God for us." Hebrews 9:9, 23; 8:5; 9:24.

The Glories of the Earthly Sanctuary and the Heavenly Temple

The sanctuary in heaven, in which Jesus ministers in our behalf, is the great original, of which the sanctuary built by Moses was a copy. . . .

The matchless splendor of the earthly tabernacle reflected to human vision the glories of that heavenly temple where Christ our forerunner ministers for us before the throne of God. The abiding place of the King of kings, where thousand thousands minister unto Him, and ten thousand times ten thousand stand before Him (Daniel 7:10); that temple, filled with the glory of the eternal throne, where seraphim, its shining guardians, veil their faces in adoration, could find, in the most magnificent structure ever reared by human hands, but a faint reflection of its vastness and glory. Yet important truths concerning the heavenly sanctuary and the great work there carried forward for man's redemption were taught by the earthly sanctuary and its services.

The holy places of the sanctuary in heaven are represented by the two apartments in the sanctuary on earth. As in vision the apostle John was granted a view of the temple of God in heaven, he beheld there "seven lamps of fire burning before the throne." Revelation 4:5. He saw an angel "having a golden censer; and there was given unto him much incense, that he should offer it with the prayers of all saints upon the golden altar which was before the throne." Revelation 8:3. Here the prophet was permitted to behold the first apartment of the sanctuary in heaven; and he saw there the "seven lamps of fire" and "the golden altar," represented by the golden candlestick and the altar of incense in the sanctuary on earth. Again, "the temple of God was opened" (Revelation 11:19), and he looked within the inner veil, upon the holy of holies. Here he beheld "the ark of His testament," represented by the sacred chest constructed by Moses to contain the law of God.

Thus those who were studying the subject found indisputable proof of the existence of a sanctuary in heaven. Moses made the earthly sanctuary after a pattern which was shown him. Paul teaches that that pattern was the true sanctuary which is in heaven. And John testifies that he saw it in heaven.

Christ's Ministry in the Heavenly Sanctuary

In the temple in heaven, the dwelling place of God, His throne is established in righteousness and judgment. In the most holy place is His law, the great rule of right by which all mankind are tested. The ark that enshrines the tables of the law is covered with the mercy seat, before which Christ pleads His blood in the sinner's behalf. Thus is represented the union of justice and mercy in the plan of human redemption. This union infinite wisdom alone could devise and infinite power accomplish; it is a union that fills all heaven with wonder and adoration. The cherubim of the earthly sanctuary, looking reverently down upon the mercy seat, represent the interest with which the heavenly host contemplate the work of redemption. This is the mystery of mercy into which angels desire to look—that God can be just while He justifies the repenting sinner and renews His intercourse with the fallen race; that Christ could stoop to raise unnumbered multitudes from the abyss of ruin and clothe them with the spotless garments of His own righteousness to unite with angels who have never fallen and to dwell forever in the presence of God.

The Glorious Temple in Heaven

The work of Christ as man's intercessor is presented in that beautiful prophecy of Zechariah concerning Him "whose name is the Branch." Says the prophet: "He shall build the temple of the Lord; and He shall bear the glory, and shall sit and rule upon His [the Father's] throne; and He shall be a priest upon His throne: and the *counsel of peace* shall be between Them both." Zechariah 6:12, 13.

"He shall build the temple of the Lord." By His sacrifice and mediation Christ is both the foundation and the builder of the church of God. The apostle Paul points to Him as "the chief Cornerstone; in whom all the building fitly framed together groweth into an holy temple in the Lord: in whom ye also," he says, "are builded together for an habitation of God through the Spirit." Ephesians 2:20-22.

"He shall bear the glory." To Christ belongs the glory of redemption for the fallen race. Through the eternal ages, the song of the ransomed ones will be: "Unto Him that loved us, and washed us from our sins in His own blood, . . . to Him be glory and dominion forever and ever." Revelation 1:5, 6.

He "shall sit and rule upon His throne; and He shall be a priest upon His throne." Not now "upon the throne of His glory;" the kingdom of glory has not yet been ushered in. Not until His work as a mediator shall be ended will God "give unto Him the throne of His father David," a kingdom of which "there shall be no end." Luke 1:32, 33. As a priest, Christ is now set down with the Father in His throne. Revelation 3:21. Upon the throne with the eternal, self-existent One is He who "hath borne our griefs, and carried our sorrows," who "was in all points tempted like as we are, yet without sin," that He might be "able to succor them that are tempted." "If any man sin, we have an advocate with the Father." Isaiah 53:4; Hebrews 4:15; 2:18; 1 John 2:1. His intercession is that of a pierced and broken body, of a spotless life. The wounded hands, the pierced side, the marred feet, plead for fallen man, whose redemption was purchased at such infinite cost.

"And the counsel of peace shall be between Them both." The love of the Father, no less than of the Son, is the fountain of salvation for the lost race. Said Jesus to His disciples before He went away: "I say not unto you, that I will pray the Father for you: for the Father Himself loveth you." John 16:26, 27. God was "in Christ, reconciling the world unto Himself." 2 Corinthians 5:19. And in the ministration in the sanctuary above, "the counsel of peace shall be between Them both." "God *so loved* the world, that He gave His only-begotten Son, that whosoever believeth in Him should not perish, but have everlasting life." John 3:16.

Determining the Sanctuary of Daniel 8:14

The question, What is the sanctuary? is clearly answered in the Scriptures. The term "sanctuary," as used in the Bible, refers, first, to the tabernacle built by Moses, as a pattern of heavenly things; and, secondly, to the "true tabernacle" in heaven, to which the earthly sanctuary pointed. At the death of Christ the typical service ended. The "true tabernacle" in heaven is the sanctuary of the new covenant. And as the prophecy of Daniel 8:14 is fulfilled in this dispensation, the sanctuary to which it refers must be the sanctuary of the new covenant. At the termination of the 2300 days, in 1844, there had been no sanctuary on earth for many centuries. Thus the prophecy, "Unto two thousand and three hundred days; then shall the sanctuary be cleansed," unquestionably points to the sanctuary in heaven.

But the most important question remains to be answered: What is the cleansing of the sanctuary? That there was such a service in connection with the earthly sanctuary is stated in the Old Testament Scriptures. But can there be anything in heaven to be cleansed? In Hebrews 9 the cleansing of both the earthly and the heavenly sanctuary is plainly taught. "Almost all things are by the law purged with blood; and without shedding of blood is no remission. It was therefore necessary that the patterns of things in the heavens should be purified with these [the blood of animals]; but the heavenly things themselves with better sacrifices than these" (Hebrews 9:22, 23), even the precious blood of Christ.

Practical Lessons From the Types

The cleansing both in the typical and in the real service, must be accomplished with blood: in the former, with the blood of animals; in the latter, with the blood of Christ. Paul states, as the reason why this cleansing must be performed with blood, that without shedding of blood is no *remission*. Remission, or putting away of sin, is the work to be accomplished. But how could there be sin connected with the sanctuary, either in heaven or upon the earth? This may be learned by reference to the symbolic service; for the priests who officiated on earth, served "unto the example and shadow of heavenly things." Hebrews 8:5.

The ministration of the earthly sanctuary consisted of two divisions; the priests ministered daily in the holy place, while once a year the high priest performed a special work of atonement in the most holy, for the cleansing of the sanctuary. Day by day the repentant sinner brought his offering to the door of the tabernacle and, placing his hand upon the victim's head, confessed his sins, thus in figure transferring them from himself to the innocent sacrifice. The animal was then slain. "Without shedding of blood," says the apostle, there is no remission of sin. "The life of the flesh is in the blood." Leviticus 17:11. The broken law of God demanded the life of the transgressor. The blood, representing the forfeited life of the sinner, whose guilt the victim bore, was carried by the priest into the holy place and sprinkled before the veil, behind which was the ark containing the law that the sinner had transgressed. By this ceremony the sin was, through the blood, transferred in figure to the sanctuary. In some cases the blood was not taken into the holy place; but the flesh was then to be eaten by the priest, as Moses directed the sons of Aaron, saying: "God hath given it you to bear the iniquity of the congregation." Leviticus 10:17. Both ceremonies alike symbolized the transfer of the sin from the penitent to the sanctuary.

Such was the work that went on, day by day, throughout the year. The sins of Israel were thus transferred to the sanctuary, and a special work became necessary for their removal. God commanded that an atonement be made for each of the sacred apartments. "He shall make an atonement for the holy place, because of the uncleanness of the children of Israel, and because of their transgressions in all their sins: and so shall he do for the tabernacle of the congregation, that remaineth among them in the midst of their uncleanness." An atonement was also to be made for the altar, to "cleanse it, and hallow it from the uncleanness of the children of Israel." Leviticus 16:16, 19.

Once a year, on the great Day of Atonement, the priest entered the most holy place for the cleansing of the sanctuary. The work there performed completed the yearly round of ministration. On the Day of Atonement two kids of the goats were brought to the door of the tabernacle, and lots were cast upon them, "one lot for the Lord, and the other lot for the scapegoat." Verse 8. The goat upon which fell the lot for the Lord was to be slain as a sin offering for the people. And the priest was to bring his blood within the veil and sprinkle it upon the mercy seat and before the mercy seat. The blood was also to be sprinkled upon the altar of incense that was before the veil.

"And Aaron shall lay both his hands upon the head of the live goat, and confess over him all the iniquities of the children of Israel, and all their transgressions in all their sins, putting them upon the head of the goat, and shall send him away by the hand of a fit man into the wilderness: and the goat shall bear upon him all their iniquities unto a land not inhabited." Verses 21, 22. The scapegoat came no more into the camp of Israel, and the man who led him away was required to wash himself and his clothing with water before returning to the camp.

The whole ceremony was designed to impress the Israelites

with the holiness of God and His abhorrence of sin; and, further, to show them that they could not come in contact with sin without becoming polluted. Every man was required to afflict his soul while this work of atonement was going forward. All business was to be laid aside, and the whole congregation of Israel were to spend the day in solemn humiliation before God, with prayer, fasting, and deep searching of heart.

Important truths concerning the atonement are taught by the typical service. A substitute was accepted in the sinner's stead; but the sin was not canceled by the blood of the victim. A means was thus provided by which it was transferred to the sanctuary. By the offering of blood the sinner acknowledged the authority of the law, confessed his guilt in transgression, and expressed his desire for pardon through faith in a Redeemer to come; but he was not yet entirely released from the condemnation of the law. On the Day of Atonement the high priest, having taken an offering from the congregation, went into the most holy place with the blood of this offering, and sprinkled it upon the mercy seat, directly over the law, to make satisfaction for its claims. Then, in his character of mediator, he took the sins upon himself and bore them from the sanctuary. Placing his hands upon the head of the scapegoat, he confessed over him all these sins, thus in figure transferring them from himself to the goat. The goat then bore them away, and they were regarded as forever separated from the people.

But a Type of Heavenly Realities

Such was the service performed "unto the example and shadow of heavenly things." And what was done in type in the ministration of the earthly sanctuary is done in reality in the ministration of the heavenly sanctuary. After His ascension our Saviour began His work as our high priest. Says Paul: "Christ is not entered into the holy places made with hands, which are the figures of the true; but into heaven itself, now to appear in the presence of God for us." Hebrews 9:24.

The ministration of the priest throughout the year in the first apartment of the sanctuary, "within the veil" which formed the door and separated the holy place from the outer court, represents the work of ministration upon which Christ entered at His ascension. It was the work of the priest in the daily ministration to present before God the blood of the sin offering, also the incense which ascended with the prayers of Israel. So did Christ plead His blood before the Father in behalf of sinners, and present before Him also, with the precious fragrance of His own righteousness, the prayers of penitent believers. Such was the work of ministration in the first apartment of the sanctuary in heaven.

Thither the faith of Christ's disciples followed Him as He ascended from their sight. Here their hopes centered, "which hope we have," said Paul, "as an anchor of the soul, both sure and steadfast, and which entereth into that within the veil; whither the forerunner is for us entered, even Jesus, made an high priest forever." "Neither by the blood of goats and calves, but by His own blood He entered in once into the holy place, having obtained eternal redemption for us." Hebrews 6:19, 20; 9:12.

The Cleansing of the Heavenly Sanctuary

For eighteen centuries this work of ministration continued in the first apartment of the sanctuary. The blood of Christ, pleaded in behalf of penitent believers, secured their pardon and acceptance with the Father, yet their sins still remained upon the books of record. As in the typical service there was a work of atonement at the close of the year, so before Christ's work for the redemption of men is completed there is a work of atonement for the removal of sin from the sanctuary. This is the service which began when the 2300 days ended. At that time, as foretold by Daniel the prophet, our High Priest entered the most holy, to perform the last division of His solemn work —to cleanse the sanctuary.

As anciently the sins of the people were by faith placed upon the sin offering and through its blood transferred, in figure, to the earthly sanctuary, so in the new covenant the sins of the repentant are by faith placed upon Christ and transferred, in fact, to the heavenly sanctuary. And as the typical cleansing of the earthly was accomplished by the removal of the sins by which it had been polluted, so the actual cleansing of the heavenly is to be accomplished by the removal, or blotting out, of the sins which are there recorded. But before this can be accomplished, there must be an examination of the books of record to determine who, through repentance of sin and faith in Christ, are entitled to the benefits of His atonement. The cleansing of the sanctuary therefore involves a work of investigation—a work of judgment. This work must be performed prior to the coming of Christ to redeem His people; for when He comes, His reward is with Him to give to every man according to his works. Revelation 22:12.

Thus those who followed in the light of the prophetic word saw that, instead of coming to the earth at the termination of the 2300 days in 1844, Christ then entered the most holy place of the heavenly sanctuary to perform the closing work of atonement preparatory to His coming.

It was seen, also, that while the sin offering pointed to Christ as a sacrifice, and the high priest represented Christ as a mediator, the scapegoat typified Satan, the author of sin, upon whom the sins of the truly penitent will finally be placed. When the high priest, by virtue of the blood of the sin offering, removed the sins from the sanctuary, he placed them upon the scapegoat. When Christ, by virtue of His own blood, removes the sins of His people from the heavenly sanctuary at the close of His ministration, He will place them upon Satan, who, in the execution of the judgment, must bear the final penalty. The scapegoat was sent away into a land not inhabited, never to come again into the congregation of Israel. So will Satan be forever banished from the presence of God and His people, and he will be blotted from existence in the final destruction of sin and sinners.—*The Great Controversy,* pages 409-422.

STUDY QUESTIONS

1. What important place did Daniel 8:14 take in the Advent faith and teaching? (87)
2. How did many of the Millerites rashly explain the disappointment? (87)
3. When the disappointed Adventists, who clung to the evidence of God's leading in their experience, could find no error in their reckoning of the prophetic periods, what did they begin to examine? (89, 90)
4. What discovery did the believers make in regard to the identity of the sanctuary? (90, 91)
5. What did they discover to be the sanctuary of the first covenant? The sanctuary of the new covenant? (90, 91)
6. What sanctuary was cleansed at the end of the 2300 days? (94)
7. What is the cleansing of the sanctuary in heaven? Why does it have to take place *before* the second coming of Christ? (94-100)
8. What is "remission of sins"? (95)
9. Note the parallel between the services of the Old Testament sanctuary and the sanctuary in heaven. (94-100)
10. By what means were the sins of the repentant sinner transferred to the heavenly sanctuary? (99)
11. Instead of coming to this earth on October 22, 1844, what did Jesus do? (99)
12. How is the sanctuary in heaven "freed, or cleansed, from the record of sin"? (99; see also 38, 39)

Our High Priest in the Holy of Holies

The subject of the sanctuary was the key which unlocked the mystery of the disappointment of 1844. It opened to view a complete system of truth, connected and harmonious, showing that God's hand had directed the great advent movement and revealing present duty as it brought to light the position and work of His people. As the disciples of Jesus after the terrible night of their anguish and disappointment were "glad when they saw the Lord," so did those now rejoice who had looked in faith for His second coming. They had expected Him to appear in glory to give reward to His servants. As their hopes were disappointed, they had lost sight of Jesus, and with Mary at the sepulcher they cried: "They have taken away my Lord, and I know not where they have laid Him." Now in the holy of holies they again beheld Him, their compassionate High Priest, soon to appear as their king and deliverer. Light from the sanctuary illumined the past, the present, and the future. They knew that God had led them by His unerring providence. Though, like the first disciples, they themselves had failed to understand the message which they bore, yet it had been in every respect correct. In proclaiming it they had fulfilled the purpose of God, and their labor had not been in vain in the Lord. Begotten "again unto a lively hope," they rejoiced "with joy unspeakable and full of glory."

Both the prophecy of Daniel 8:14, "Unto two thousand and three hundred days; then shall the sanctuary be cleansed," and the first angel's message, "Fear God, and give glory to Him; for the hour of His judgment is come," pointed to Christ's ministration in the most holy place, to the investigative judgment, and not to the coming of Christ for the redemption of His people and the destruction of the wicked. The mistake had not been in the reckoning of the prophetic periods, but in the *event* to take place at the end of the 2300 days. Through this error the believers had suffered disappointment, yet all that was foretold by the prophecy, and all that they had any Scripture warrant to expect, had been accomplished. At the very time when they were lamenting the failure of their hopes, the event had taken place which was foretold by the message, and which must be fulfilled before the Lord could appear to give reward to His servants.

Christ had come, not to the earth, as they expected, but, as foreshadowed in the type, to the most holy place of the temple of God in heaven. He is represented by the prophet Daniel as coming at this time to the Ancient of Days: "I saw in the night visions, and, behold, one like the Son of man came with the clouds of heaven, and came"—not to the earth, but—"to the Ancient of Days, and they brought Him near before Him." Daniel 7:13.

This coming is foretold also by the prophet Malachi: "The Lord, whom ye seek, shall suddenly come to His temple, even the Messenger of the covenant, whom ye delight in: behold, He shall come, saith the Lord of hosts." Malachi 3:1. The coming of the Lord to His temple was sudden, unexpected, to His people. They were not looking for Him *there*. They expected Him to come to earth, "in flaming fire taking vengeance on them that know not God, and that obey not the gospel." 2 Thessalonians 1:8.

But the people were not yet ready to meet their Lord. There was still a work of preparation to be accomplished for them. Light was to be given, directing their minds to the temple of God in heaven; and as they should by faith follow their High Priest in His ministration there, new duties would be revealed.

Another message of warning and instruction was to be given to the church.

Says the prophet: "Who may abide the day of His coming? and who shall stand when He appeareth? for He is like a refiner's fire, and like fullers' soap: and He shall sit as a refiner and purifier of silver: and He shall purify the sons of Levi, and purge them as gold and silver, that they may offer unto the Lord an offering in righteousness." Malachi 3:2, 3. Those who are living upon the earth when the intercession of Christ shall cease in the sanctuary above are to stand in the sight of a holy God without a mediator. Their robes must be spotless, their characters must be purified from sin by the blood of sprinkling. Through the grace of God and their own diligent effort they must be conquerors in the battle with evil. While the investigative judgment is going forward in heaven, while the sins of penitent believers are being removed from the sanctuary, there is to be a special work of purification, of putting away of sin, among God's people upon earth. This work is more clearly presented in the messages of Revelation 14.

When this work shall have been accomplished, the followers of Christ will be ready for His appearing. "Then shall the offering of Judah and Jerusalem be pleasant unto the Lord, as in the days of old, and as in former years." Malachi 3:4. Then the church which our Lord at His coming is to receive to Himself will be a "glorious church, not having spot, or wrinkle, or any such thing." Ephesians 5:27. Then she will look "forth as the morning, fair as the moon, clear as the sun, and terrible as an army with banners." Song of Solomon 6:10.

Besides the coming of the Lord to His temple, Malachi also foretells His second advent, His coming for the execution of the judgment, in these words: "And I will come near to you to judgment; and I will be a swift witness against the sorcerers, and against the adulterers, and against false swearers, and against those that oppress the hireling in his wages, the widow, and the fatherless, and that turn aside the stranger from his right, and fear not Me, saith the Lord of hosts." Malachi 3:5. Jude refers to the same scene when he says, "Behold, the Lord cometh with ten thousands of His saints, to execute judgment upon all, and to convince all that are ungodly among them of all their ungodly deeds." Jude 14, 15. This coming, and the coming of the Lord to His temple, are distinct and separate events.

Scriptural Foundations

The coming of Christ as our high priest to the most holy place, for the cleansing of the sanctuary, brought to view in Daniel 8:14; the coming of the Son of man to the Ancient of Days, as presented in Daniel 7:13; and the coming of the Lord to His temple, foretold by Malachi, are descriptions of the same event; and this is also represented by the coming of the bridegroom to the marriage, described by Christ in the parable of the ten virgins, of Matthew 25.

In the summer and autumn of 1844 the proclamation, "Behold, the Bridegroom cometh," was given. The two classes represented by the wise and foolish virgins were then developed—one class who looked with joy to the Lord's appearing, and who had been diligently preparing to meet Him; another class that, influenced by fear and acting from impulse, had been satisfied with a theory of the truth, but were destitute of the grace of God. In the parable, when the bridegroom came, "they that were ready went in with him to the marriage." The coming of the bridegroom, here brought to view, takes place before the marriage. The marriage represents the reception by Christ of His kingdom. The Holy City, the New Jerusalem, which is the capital and representative of the kingdom, is called "the bride, the Lamb's wife." Said the angel to John: "Come hither, I will show thee the bride, the Lamb's wife." "He carried me away in the spirit," says the prophet, "and showed me that great city, the holy Jerusalem, descending out of heaven from God." Revelation 21:9, 10. Clearly, then, the bride represents the Holy City, and the virgins that go out to meet the bridegroom are a symbol of the church. In the Revelation the people of God are said to be the guests at the marriage supper. Revelation 19:9. If *guests*, they cannot be represented also as the *bride*. Christ, as stated by the prophet Daniel, will receive from the Ancient of Days in heaven, "dominion, and glory, and a kingdom;" He will receive the New Jerusalem, the capital of His kingdom, "prepared as a bride adorned for her husband." Daniel 7:14; Revelation 21:2. Having received the kingdom, He will come in His glory, as King of kings and Lord of lords, for the redemption of His people, who are to "sit down with Abraham, and Isaac, and Jacob," at His table in His kingdom (Matthew 8:11; Luke 22:30), to partake of the marriage supper of the Lamb.

The proclamation, "Behold, the Bridegroom cometh," in the summer of 1844, led thousands to expect the immediate advent of the Lord. At the appointed time the Bridegroom came, not to the earth, as the people expected, but to the Ancient of Days in heaven, to the marriage, the reception of His kingdom. "They that were ready went in with Him to the marriage: and the door was shut." They were not to be present in person at the marriage; for it takes place in heaven, while they are upon the earth. The followers of Christ are to "wait for their Lord, when He will *return from* the wedding." Luke 12:36. But they are to understand His work, and to follow Him by faith as He goes in before God. It is in this sense that they are said to go in to the marriage.

In the parable it was those that had oil in their vessels with their lamps that went in to the marriage. Those who, with a knowledge of the truth from the Scriptures, had also the Spirit and grace of God, and who, in the night of their bitter trial, had patiently waited, searching the Bible for clearer light—these saw the truth concerning the sanctuary in heaven and the Saviour's change in ministration, and by faith they followed Him in His work in the sanctuary above. And all who through the testimony of the Scriptures accept the same truths, following Christ by faith as He enters in before God to perform the last work of mediation, and at its close to receive His kingdom—all these are represented as going in to the marriage.

In the parable of Matthew 22 the same figure of the marriage is introduced, and the investigative judgment is clearly represented as taking place before the marriage. Previous to the wedding the king comes in to see the guests, to see if all are attired in the wedding garment, the spotless robe of character washed and made white in the blood of the Lamb. Matthew 22:11; Revelation 7:14. He who is found wanting is cast out, but all who upon examination are seen to have the wedding garment on are accepted of God and accounted worthy of a share in His kingdom and a seat upon His throne. This work of examination of character, of determining who are prepared for the kingdom of God, is that of the investigative judgment, the closing work in the sanctuary above.

When the work of investigation shall be ended, when the cases of those who in all ages have professed to be followers of Christ have been examined and decided, then, and not till then, probation will close, and the door of mercy will be shut. Thus in the one short sentence, "They that were ready went in with Him to the marriage: and the door was shut," we are carried down through the Saviour's final ministration, to the time when the great work for man's salvation shall be completed.

Ministry in the Two Apartments

In the service of the earthly sanctuary, which, as we have seen, is a figure of the service in the heavenly, when the high priest on the Day of Atonement entered the most holy place, the ministration in the first apartment ceased. God commanded: "There shall be no man in the tabernacle of the congregation when he goeth in to make an atonement in the holy place, until he comes out." Leviticus 16:17. So when Christ entered the holy of holies to perform the closing work of the atonement, He ceased His ministration in the first apartment. But when the ministration in the first apartment ended, the ministration in the second apartment began. When in the typical service the high priest left the holy on the Day of Atonement, he went in before God to present the blood of the sin offering in behalf of all Israel who truly repented of their sins. So Christ had only completed one part of His work as our intercessor, to enter upon another portion of the work, and He still pleaded His blood before the Father in behalf of sinners.

This subject was not understood by Adventists in 1844. After the passing of the time when the Saviour was expected, they still believed His coming to be near; they held that they had reached an important crisis and that the work of Christ as man's intercessor before God had ceased. It appeared to them to be taught in the Bible that man's probation would close a short time before the actual coming of the Lord in the clouds of heaven. This seemed evident from those scriptures which point to a time when men will seek, knock, and cry at the door of mercy, and it will not be opened. And it was a question with them whether the date to which they had looked for the coming of Christ might not rather mark the beginning of this period which was immediately to precede His coming. Having given the warning of the judgment near, they felt that their work for the world was done, and they lost their burden of soul for the salvation of sinners, while the bold and blasphemous scoffing of the ungodly seemed to them another evidence that the Spirit of God had been withdrawn from the rejecters of His mercy. All this confirmed them in the belief that probation had ended, or, as they then expressed it, "the door of mercy was shut."

The Opening of Another Door

But clearer light came with the investigation of the sanctuary question. They now saw that they were correct in believing that the end of the 2300 days in 1844 marked an important crisis. But while it was true that that door of hope and mercy by which men had for eighteen hundred years found access to God, was closed, another door was opened, and forgiveness of sins was offered to men through the intercession of Christ in the most holy. One part of His ministration had closed, only to give place to another. There was still an "open door" to the heavenly sanctuary, where Christ was ministering in the sinner's behalf.

Now was seen the application of those words of Christ in the Revelation, addressed to the church at this very time: "These things saith He that is holy, He that is true, He that hath the key of David, He that openeth, and no man shutteth; and shutteth, and no man openeth; I know thy works: behold, I have set before thee an open door, and no man can shut it." Revelation 3:7, 8.

It is those who by faith follow Jesus in the great work of the atonement who receive the benefits of His mediation in their behalf, while those who reject the light which brings to view this work of ministration are not benefited thereby. The Jews who rejected the light given at Christ's first advent, and refused to believe on Him as the Saviour of the world, could not receive pardon through Him. When Jesus at His ascension entered by His own blood into the heavenly sanctuary to shed upon His disciples the blessings of His mediation, the Jews were left in total darkness to continue their useless sacrifices and offerings. The ministration of types and shadows had ceased. That door by which men had formerly found access to God was no longer open. The Jews had refused to seek Him in the only way whereby He could then be found, through the ministration in the sanctuary in heaven. Therefore they found no communion with God. To them the door was shut. They had no knowledge of Christ as the true sacrifice and the only mediator before God; hence they could not receive the benefits of His mediation.

The condition of the unbelieving Jews illustrates the condition of the careless and unbelieving among professed Christians, who are willingly ignorant of the work of our merciful High Priest. In the typical service, when the high priest entered the most holy place, all Israel were required to gather about the sanctuary and in the most solemn manner humble their souls before God, that they might receive the pardon of their sins and not be cut off from the congregation. How much more essential in this antitypical Day of Atonement that we understand the work of our High Priest and know what duties are required of us.

The Tragic Result of Rejecting God's Warning Message

Men cannot with impunity reject the warning which God in mercy sends them. A message was sent from heaven to the world in Noah's day, and their salvation depended upon the manner in which they treated that message. Because they rejected the warning, the Spirit of God was withdrawn from the sinful race, and they perished in the waters of the Flood. In the time of Abraham, mercy ceased to plead with the guilty inhabitants of Sodom, and all but Lot with his wife and two daughters were consumed by the fire sent down from heaven. So in the days of Christ. The Son of God declared to the unbelieving Jews of that generation: "Your house is left unto you desolate." Matthew 23:38. Looking down to the last days, the same Infinite Power declares, concerning those who "received not the love of the truth, that they might be saved": "For this cause God shall send them strong delusion, that they should believe a lie: that they all might be damned who believed not the truth, but had pleasure in unrighteousness." 2 Thessalonians 2:10-12. As they reject the teachings of His word, God withdraws His Spirit and leaves them to the deceptions which they love.

But Christ still intercedes in man's behalf, and light will be given to those who seek it. Though this was not at first understood by Adventists, it was afterward made plain as the Scriptures which define their true position began to open before them.

The passing of the time in 1844 was followed by a period of great trial to those who still held the advent faith. Their only relief, so far as ascertaining their true position was concerned, was the light which directed their minds to the sanctuary above. Some renounced their faith in their former reckoning of the prophetic periods and ascribed to human or satanic agencies the powerful influence of the Holy Spirit which had attended the advent movement. Another class firmly held that the Lord had led them in their past experience; and as they waited and watched and prayed to know the will of God they saw that their great High Priest had entered upon another work of ministration, and, following Him by faith, they were led to see also the closing work of the church. They had a clearer understanding of the first and second angels' messages, and were prepared to receive and give to the world the solemn warning of the third angel of Revelation 14.—*The Great Controversy,* pages 423-432.

The Sanctuary and the Sabbath

"The temple of God was opened in heaven, and there was seen in His temple the ark of His testament." Revelation 11:19. The ark of God's testament is in the holy of holies, the second apartment of the sanctuary. In the ministration of the earthly tabernacle, which served "unto the example and shadow of heavenly things," this apartment was opened only upon the great Day of Atonement for the cleansing of the sanctuary. Therefore the announcement that the temple of God was opened in heaven and the ark of His testament was seen points to the opening of the most holy place of the heavenly sanctuary in 1844 as Christ entered there to perform the closing work of the atonement. Those who by faith followed their great High Priest as He entered upon His ministry in the most holy place, beheld the ark of His testament. As they had studied the subject of the sanctuary they had come to understand the Saviour's change of ministration, and they saw that He was now officiating before the ark of God, pleading His blood in behalf of sinners.

The ark in the tabernacle on earth contained the two tables of stone, upon which were inscribed the precepts of the law of God. The ark was merely a receptacle for the tables of the law, and the presence of these divine precepts gave to it its value and sacredness. When the temple of God was opened in heaven, the ark of His testament was seen. Within the holy of holies, in the sanctuary in heaven, the divine law is sacredly enshrined

—the law that was spoken by God Himself amid the thunders of Sinai and written with His own finger on the tables of stone.

The law of God in the sanctuary in heaven is the great original, of which the precepts inscribed upon the tables of stone and recorded by Moses in the Pentateuch were an unerring transcript. Those who arrived at an understanding of this important point were thus led to see the sacred, unchanging character of the divine law. They saw, as never before, the force of the Saviour's words: "Till heaven and earth pass, one jot or one tittle shall in no wise pass from the law." Matthew 5:18. The law of God, being a revelation of His will, a transcript of His character, must forever endure, "as a faithful witness in heaven." Not one command has been annulled; not a jot or tittle has been changed. Says the psalmist: "Forever, O Lord, Thy word is settled in heaven." "All His commandments are sure. They stand fast for ever and ever." Psalms 119:89; 111:7, 8.

In the very bosom of the Decalogue is the fourth commandment, as it was first proclaimed: "Remember the Sabbath day, to keep it holy. Six days shalt thou labor, and do all thy work: but the seventh day is the Sabbath of the Lord thy God: in it thou shalt not do any work, thou, nor thy son, nor thy daughter, thy manservant, nor thy maidservant, nor thy cattle, nor thy stranger that is within thy gates: for in six days the Lord made heaven and earth, the sea, and all that in them is, and rested the seventh day: wherefore the Lord blessed the Sabbath day, and hallowed it." Exodus 20:8-11.

The Spirit of God impressed the hearts of those students of His word. The conviction was urged upon them that they had ignorantly transgressed this precept by disregarding the Creator's rest day. They began to examine the reasons for observing the first day of the week instead of the day which God had sanctified. They could find no evidence in the Scriptures that the fourth commandment had been abolished, or that the Sabbath had been changed; the blessing which first hallowed the seventh day had never been removed. They had been honestly seeking to know and to do God's will; now, as they saw themselves transgressors of His law, sorrow filled their hearts, and they manifested their loyalty to God by keeping His Sabbath holy.

Many and earnest were the efforts made to overthrow their faith. None could fail to see that if the earthly sanctuary was a figure or pattern of the heavenly, the law deposited in the ark on earth was an exact transcript of the law in the ark in heaven; and that an acceptance of the truth concerning the heavenly sanctuary involved an acknowledgment of the claims of God's law and the obligation of the Sabbath of the fourth commandment. Here was the secret of the bitter and determined opposition to the harmonious exposition of the Scriptures that revealed the ministration of Christ in the heavenly sanctuary. Men sought to close the door which God had opened, and to open the door which He had closed. But "He that openeth, and no man shutteth; and shutteth, and no man openeth," had declared: "Behold, I have set before thee an open door, and no man can shut it." Revelation 3:7, 8. Christ had opened the door, or ministration, of the most holy place, light was shining from that open door of the sanctuary in heaven, and the fourth commandment was shown to be included in the law which is there enshrined; what God had established, no man could overthrow.

Those who had accepted the light concerning the mediation of Christ and the perpetuity of the law of God found that these were the truths presented in Revelation 14. The messages of this chapter constitute a threefold warning which is to prepare the inhabitants of the earth for the Lord's second coming. The announcement, "The hour of His judgment is come," points to the closing work of Christ's ministration for the salvation of men. It heralds a truth which must be proclaimed until the Saviour's intercession shall cease and He shall return to the earth to take His people to Himself. The work of judgment which began in 1844 must continue until the cases of all are decided, both of the living and the dead; hence it will extend to the close of human probation. That men may be prepared to stand in the judgment, the message commands them to "fear God, and give glory to Him," "and worship Him that made heaven, and earth, and the sea, and the fountains of waters." The result of an acceptance of these messages is given in the word: "Here are they that keep the commandments of God, and the faith of Jesus." In order to be prepared for the judgment, it is necessary that men should keep the law of God. That law will be the standard of character in the judgment.—*The Great Controversy*, pages 433-436.

Those who received the light concerning the sanctuary and the immutability of the law of God were filled with joy and wonder as they saw the beauty and harmony of the system of truth that opened to their understanding.—*Ibid.*, p. 454.

STUDY QUESTIONS

1. What was the key that unlocked the mystery of the 1844 disappointment? (101)
2. Quote the *two* Bible texts that point to Christ's ministration in the most holy place. (101, 102)
3. Which "coming" of Christ is depicted in Daniel 7:13 and Malachi 3:1? (102)
4. While the sins of penitent believers are being removed from heaven's sanctuary, what are these same believers to be doing on earth? (103)
5. The wise and foolish virgins represent what *two* classes among advent believers of the summer and autumn of 1844? (104)
6. What is the bride of Christ? (104, 105)
7. Who are the "guests" at the wedding? (104, 105)
8. How does the parable of Matthew 22 picture the work of judgment? (106)
9. Why did Adventists for a time after the disappointment lose their burden for the salvation of sinners? (107)
10. What, then, was the Adventist interpretation of the "shut door" immediately after the disappointment? (107)
11. What later was found to be the "open door," and who opened it? (107, 108)
12. As the temple in heaven was opened, what was revealed? (110)
13. What relationship exists between the law of God enshrined in the heavenly sanctuary and the law deposited in the ark in the earthly sanctuary? (111)
14. With this revelation of God's law to what did earnest Bible study lead? (111-113)

Christ's Closing Ministry in the Heavenly Sanctuary

The preaching of a definite time for the judgment, in the giving of the first message, was ordered of God. The computation of the prophetic periods on which that message was based, placing the close of the 2300 days in the autumn of 1844, stands without impeachment.—*The Great Controversy,* page 457.

"I beheld," says the prophet Daniel, "till thrones were placed, and One that was Ancient of Days did sit: His raiment was white as snow, and the hair of His head like pure wool; His throne was fiery flames, and the wheels thereof burning fire. A fiery stream issued and came forth from before Him: thousand thousands ministered unto Him, and ten thousand times ten thousand stood before Him: the judgment was set, and the books were opened." Daniel 7:9, 10, R.V.

Thus was presented to the prophet's vision the great and solemn day when the characters and the lives of men should pass in review before the Judge of all the earth, and to every man should be rendered "according to his works." The Ancient of Days is God the Father. Says the psalmist: "Before the mountains were brought forth, or ever Thou hadst formed the earth and the world, even from everlasting to everlasting, Thou art God." Psalm 90:2. It is He, the source of all being, and the fountain of all law, that is to preside in the judgment. And holy angels as ministers and witnesses, in number "ten thousand times ten thousand, and thousands of thousands," attend this great tribunal.

"And, behold, one like the Son of man came with the clouds of heaven, and came to the Ancient of Days, and they brought Him near before Him. And there was given Him dominion, and glory, and a kingdom, that all people, nations, and languages, should serve Him: His dominion is an everlasting dominion, which shall not pass away." Daniel 7:13, 14. The coming of Christ here described is not His second coming to the earth. He comes to the Ancient of Days in heaven to receive dominion and glory and a kingdom, which will be given Him at the close of His work as a mediator. It is this coming, and not His second advent to the earth, that was foretold in prophecy to take place at the termination of the 2300 days in 1844. Attended by heavenly angels, our great High Priest enters the holy of holies and there appears in the presence of God to engage in the last acts of His ministration in behalf of man—to perform the work of investigative judgment and to make an atonement for all who are shown to be entitled to its benefits.

Whose Cases Considered?

In the typical service only those who had come before God with confession and repentance, and whose sins, through the blood of the sin offering, were transferred to the sanctuary, had a part in the service of the Day of Atonement. So in the great day of final atonement and investigative judgment the only cases considered are those of the professed people of God. The judgment of the wicked is a distinct and separate work, and takes place at a later period. "Judgment must begin at the house of God: and if it first begin at us, what shall the end be of them that obey not the gospel?" 1 Peter 4:17.

The books of record in heaven, in which the names and the deeds of men are registered, are to determine the decisions of the judgment. Says the prophet Daniel: "The judgment was set, and the books were opened." The revelator, describing the same scene, adds: "Another book was opened, which is the book of life: and the dead were judged out of those things which were written in the books, according to their works." Revelation 20:12.

The book of life contains the names of all who have ever entered the service of God. Jesus bade His disciples: "Rejoice, because your names are written in heaven." Luke 10:20. Paul speaks of his faithful fellow workers, "whose names are in the book of life." Philippians 4:3. Daniel, looking down to "a time of trouble, such as never was," declares that God's people shall be delivered, "everyone that shall be found written in the book." And the revelator says that those only shall enter the city of God whose names "are written in the Lamb's book of life." Daniel 12:1; Revelation 21:27.

"A book of remembrance" is written before God, in which are recorded the good deeds of "them that feared the Lord, and that thought upon His name." Malachi 3:16. Their words of faith, their acts of love, are registered in heaven. Nehemiah refers to this when he says: "Remember me, O my God, . . . and wipe not out my good deeds that I have done for the house of my God." Nehemiah 13:14. In the book of God's remembrance every deed of righteousness is immortalized. There every temptation resisted, every evil overcome, every word of tender pity expressed, is faithfully chronicled. And every act of sacrifice, every suffering and sorrow endured for Christ's sake, is recorded. Says the psalmist: "Thou tellest my wanderings: put Thou my tears into Thy bottle: are they not in Thy book?" Psalm 56:8.

There is a record also of the sins of men. "For God shall bring every work into judgment, with every secret thing, whether it be good, or whether it be evil." "Every idle word that men shall speak, they shall give account thereof in the day of judgment." Says the Saviour: "By thy words thou shalt be justified, and by thy words thou shalt be condemned." Ecclesiastes 12:14; Matthew 12:36, 37. The secret purposes and motives appear in the unerring register; for God "will bring to light the hidden things of darkness, and will make manifest the counsels of the hearts." 1 Corinthians 4:5. "Behold, it is written before Me, . . . your iniquities, and the iniquities of your fathers together, saith the Lord." Isaiah 65:6, 7.

Every man's work passes in review before God and is registered for faithfulness or unfaithfulness. Opposite each name in the books of heaven is entered with terrible exactness every wrong word, every selfish act, every unfulfilled duty, and every secret sin, with every artful dissembling. Heaven-sent warnings or reproofs neglected, wasted moments, unimproved opportunities, the influence exerted for good or for evil, with its far-reaching results, all are chronicled by the recording angel.

God's Law the Standard

The law of God is the standard by which the characters and the lives of men will be tested in the judgment. Says the wise man: "Fear God, and keep His commandments: for this is the whole duty of man. For God shall bring every work into judgment." Ecclesiastes 12:13, 14. The apostle James admonishes his brethren: "So speak ye, and so do, as they that shall be judged by the law of liberty." James 2:12.

Those who in the judgment are "accounted worthy" will have a part in the resurrection of the just. Jesus said: "They which shall be accounted worthy to obtain that world, and the resurrection from the dead, . . . are equal unto the angels; and are the children of God, being the children of the resurrection." Luke 20:35, 36. And again He declares that "they that have done good" shall come forth "unto the resurrection of life." John 5:29. The righteous dead will not be raised until after the judgment at which they are accounted worthy of "the resurrection of life." Hence they will not be present in person at the tribunal when their records are examined and their cases decided.

Jesus the Advocate

Jesus will appear as their advocate, to plead in their behalf before God. "If any man sin, we have an advocate with the Father, Jesus Christ the righteous." 1 John 2:1. "For Christ is not entered into the holy places made with hands, which are the figures of the true; but into heaven itself, now to appear in the presence of God for us." "Wherefore He is able also to save them to the uttermost that come unto God by Him, seeing He ever liveth to make intercession for them." Hebrews 9:24; 7:25.

As the books of record are opened in the judgment, the lives of all who have believed on Jesus come in review before God. Beginning with those who first lived upon the earth, our Advocate presents the cases of each successive generation, and closes with the living. Every name is mentioned, every case closely investigated. Names are accepted, names rejected. When any have sins remaining upon the books of record, unrepented of and unforgiven, their names will be blotted out of the book of life, and the record of their good deeds will be erased from the book of God's remembrance. The Lord declared to Moses: "Whosoever hath sinned against Me, him will I blot out of My book." Exodus 32:33. And says the prophet Ezekiel: "When the righteous turneth away from his righteousness, and committeth iniquity, . . . all his righteousness that he hath done shall not be mentioned." Ezekiel 18:24.

All who have truly repented of sin, and by faith claimed the blood of Christ as their atoning sacrifice, have had pardon entered against their names in the books of heaven; as they have become partakers of the righteousness of Christ, and their characters are found to be in harmony with the law of God, their sins will be blotted out, and they themselves will be accounted worthy of eternal life. The Lord declares, by the prophet Isaiah: "I, even I, am He that blotteth out thy transgressions for Mine own sake, and will not remember thy sins." Isaiah 43:25. Said Jesus: "He that overcometh, the same shall be clothed in white raiment; and I will not blot out his name out of the book of life, but I will confess his name before My Father, and before His angels." "Whosoever therefore shall confess Me before men, him will I confess also before My Father which is in heaven. But whosoever shall deny Me before men, him will I also deny before My Father which is in heaven." Revelation 3:5; Matthew 10:32, 33.

The Courtroom Scene

The deepest interest manifested among men in the decisions of earthly tribunals but faintly represents the interest evinced in the heavenly courts when the names entered in the book of life come up in review before the Judge of all the earth. The divine Intercessor presents the plea that all who have overcome through faith in His blood be forgiven their transgressions, that they be restored to their Eden home, and crowned as joint heirs with Himself to "the first dominion." Micah 4:8. Satan in his efforts to deceive and tempt our race had thought to frustrate the divine plan in man's creation; but Christ now asks that this plan be carried into effect as if man had never fallen. He asks for His people not only pardon and justification, full and complete, but a share in His glory and a seat upon His throne.

While Jesus is pleading for the subjects of His grace, Satan accuses them before God as transgressors. The great deceiver has sought to lead them into skepticism, to cause them to lose confidence in God, to separate themselves from His love, and to break His law. Now he points to the record of their lives, to the defects of character, the unlikeness to Christ, which has dishonored their Redeemer, to all the sins that he has tempted them to commit, and because of these he claims them as his subjects.

Jesus does not excuse their sins, but shows their penitence and faith, and, claiming for them forgiveness, He lifts His wounded hands before the Father and the holy angels, saying: I know them by name. I have graven them on the palms of My hands. "The sacrifices of God are a broken spirit: a broken and a contrite heart, O God, Thou wilt not despise." Psalm 51:17. And to the accuser of His people He declares: "The Lord rebuke thee, O Satan; even the Lord that hath chosen Jerusalem rebuke thee: is not this a brand plucked out of the fire?" Zechariah 3:2. Christ will clothe His faithful ones with His own righteousness, that He may present them to His Father "a glorious church, not having spot, or wrinkle, or any such thing." Ephesians 5:27. Their names stand enrolled in the book of life, and concerning them it is written: "They shall walk with Me in white: for they are worthy." Revelation 3:4.

Thus will be realized the complete fulfillment of the new-covenant promise: "I will forgive their iniquity, and I will remember their sin no more." "In those days, and in that time, saith the Lord, the iniquity of Israel shall be sought for, and there shall be none; and the sins of Judah, and they shall not be found." Jeremiah 31:34; 50:20. "In that day shall the branch of the Lord be beautiful and glorious, and the fruit of the earth shall be excellent and comely for them that are escaped of Israel. And it shall come to pass, that he that is left in Zion, and he that remaineth in Jerusalem, shall be called holy, even everyone that is written among the living in Jerusalem." Isaiah 4:2, 3.

The work of the investigative judgment and the blotting out of sins is to be accomplished before the second advent of the Lord. Since the dead are to be judged out of the things written in the books, it is impossible that the sins of men should be blotted out until after the judgment at which their cases are to be investigated. But the apostle Peter distinctly states that the sins of believers will be blotted out "when the times of refreshing shall come from the presence of the Lord; and He shall send Jesus Christ." Acts 3:19, 20. When the investigative judgment closes, Christ will come, and His reward will be with Him to give to every man as his work shall be.

The Closing Scenes of the Antitypical Service

In the typical service the high priest, having made the atonement for Israel, came forth and blessed the congregation. So Christ, at the close of His work as mediator, will appear, "without sin unto salvation" (Hebrews 9:28), to bless His waiting people with eternal life. As the priest, in removing the sins from the sanctuary, confessed them upon the head of the scapegoat, so Christ will place all these sins upon Satan, the originator and instigator of sin. The scapegoat, bearing the sins of Israel, was sent away "unto a land not inhabited" (Leviticus 16:22); so Satan, bearing the guilt of all the sins which he has caused God's people to commit, will be for a thousand years confined to the earth, which will then be desolate, without inhabitant, and he will at last suffer the full penalty of sin in the fires that shall destroy all the wicked. Thus the great plan of redemption will reach its accomplishment in the final eradication of sin and the deliverance of all who have been willing to renounce evil.

Judged by the Unerring Records

At the time appointed for the judgment—the close of the 2300 days, in 1844—began the work of investigation and blotting out of sins. All who have ever taken upon themselves the name of Christ must pass its searching scrutiny. Both the living and the dead are to be judged "out of those things which were written in the books, according to their works."

Sins that have not been repented of and forsaken will not be pardoned and blotted out of the books of record, but will stand to witness against the sinner in the day of God. He may have committed his evil deeds in the light of day or in the darkness of night; but they were open and manifest before Him with whom we have to do. Angels of God witnessed each sin and registered it in the unerring records. Sin may be concealed, denied, covered up from father, mother, wife, children, and associates; no one but the guilty actors may cherish the least suspicion of the wrong; but it is laid bare before the intelligences of heaven. The darkness of the darkest night, the secrecy of all deceptive arts, is not sufficient to veil one thought from the knowledge of the Eternal. God has an exact record of every unjust account and every unfair dealing. He is not deceived by appearances of piety. He makes no mistakes in His estimation of character. Men may be deceived by those who are corrupt in heart, but God pierces all disguises and reads the inner life.

How solemn is the thought! Day after day, passing into eternity, bears its burden of records for the books of heaven. Words once spoken, deeds once done, can never be recalled. Angels have registered both the good and the evil. The mightiest conqueror upon the earth cannot call back the record of even a single day. Our acts, our words, even our most secret motives, all have their weight in deciding our destiny for weal or woe. Though they may be forgotten by us, they will bear their testimony to justify or condemn.

As the features of the countenance are reproduced with unerring accuracy on the polished plate of the artist, so the character is faithfully delineated in the books above. Yet how little solicitude is felt concerning that record which is to meet the gaze of heavenly beings. Could the veil which separates the visible from the invisible world be swept back, and the children of men behold an angel recording every word and deed, which they must meet again in the judgment, how many words that are daily uttered would remain unspoken, how many deeds would remain undone.

In the judgment the use made of every talent will be scrutinized. How have we employed the capital lent us of Heaven? Will the Lord at His coming receive His own with usury? Have we improved the powers entrusted us, in hand and heart and brain, to the glory of God and the blessing of the world? How have we used our time, our pen, our voice, our money, our influence? What have we done for Christ, in the person of the poor, the afflicted, the orphan, or the widow? God has made us the depositaries of His holy word; what have we done with the light and truth given us to make men wise unto salvation? No value is attached to a mere profession of faith in Christ; only the love which is shown by works is counted genuine. Yet it is love alone which in the sight of Heaven makes any act of value. Whatever is done from love, however small it may appear in the estimation of men, is accepted and rewarded of God.

The hidden selfishness of men stands revealed in the books of heaven. There is the record of unfulfilled duties to their fellow men, of forgetfulness of the Saviour's claims. There they will see how often were given to Satan the time, thought, and strength that belonged to Christ. Sad is the record which angels bear to heaven. Intelligent beings, professed followers of Christ, are absorbed in the acquirement of worldly possessions or the enjoyment of earthly pleasures. Money, time, and strength are sacrificed for display and self-indulgence; but few are the moments devoted to prayer, to the searching of the Scriptures, to humiliation of soul and confession of sin.

Satan invents unnumbered schemes to occupy our minds, that they may not dwell upon the very work with which we ought to be best acquainted. The archdeceiver hates the great truths that bring to view an atoning sacrifice and an all-powerful mediator. He knows that with him everything depends on his diverting minds from Jesus and His truth.

Perfecting Holiness in the Fear of God

Those who would share the benefits of the Saviour's mediation should permit nothing to interfere with their duty to perfect holiness in the fear of God. The precious hours, instead of being given to pleasure, to display, or to gain seeking, should be devoted to an earnest, prayerful study of the word of truth. The subject of the sanctuary and the investigative judgment should be clearly understood by the people of God. All need a knowledge for themselves of the position and work of their great High Priest. Otherwise it will be impossible for them to exercise the faith which is essential at this time or to occupy the position which God designs them to fill. Every individual has a soul to save or to lose. Each has a case pending at the bar of God. Each must meet the great judge face to face. How important, then, that every mind contemplate often the solemn scene when the judgment shall sit and the books shall be opened, when, with Daniel, every individual must stand in his lot, at the end of the days.

All who have received the light upon these subjects are to bear testimony of the great truths which God has committed to them. The sanctuary in heaven is the very center of Christ's work in behalf of men. It concerns every soul living upon the earth. It opens to view the plan of redemption, bringing us down to the very close of time and revealing the triumphant issue of the contest between righteousness and sin. It is of the utmost importance that all should thoroughly investigate these subjects and be able to give an answer to everyone that asketh them a reason of the hope that is in them.

The intercession of Christ in man's behalf in the sanctuary above is as essential to the plan of salvation as was His death upon the cross. By His death He began that work which after His resurrection He ascended to complete in heaven. We must by faith enter within the veil, "whither the forerunner is for us entered." Hebrews 6:20. There the light from the cross of Calvary is reflected. There we may gain a clearer insight into the mysteries of redemption. The salvation of man is accomplished at an infinite expense to heaven; the sacrifice made is equal to the broadest demands of the broken law of God. Jesus has opened the way to the Father's throne, and through His mediation the sincere desire of all who come to Him in faith may be presented before God.

"He that covereth his sins shall not prosper: but whoso confesseth and forsaketh them shall have mercy." Proverbs 28:13. If those who hide and excuse their faults could see how Satan exults over them, how he taunts Christ and holy angels with their course, they would make haste to confess their sins and to put them away. Through defects in the character, Satan works to gain control of the whole mind, and he knows that if these defects are cherished, he will succeed. Therefore he is constantly seeking to deceive the followers of Christ with his fatal sophistry that it is impossible for them to overcome. But Jesus pleads in their behalf His wounded hands, His bruised body; and He declares to all who would follow Him: "My grace is sufficient for thee." 2 Corinthians 12:9. "Take My yoke upon you, and learn of Me; for I am meek and lowly in heart: and ye shall find rest unto your souls. For My yoke is easy, and My burden is light." Matthew 11:29, 30. Let none, then, regard their defects as incurable. God will give faith and grace to overcome them.

Now in the Day of Atonement

We are now living in the great day of atonement. In the typical service, while the high priest was making the atonement for Israel, all were required to afflict their souls by repentance of sin and humiliation before the Lord, lest they be cut off from among the people. In like manner, all who would have their names retained in the book of life should now, in the few remaining days of their probation, afflict their souls before God by sorrow for sin and true repentance. There must be deep, faithful searching of heart. The light, frivolous spirit indulged by so many professed Christians must be put away. There is earnest warfare before all who would subdue the evil tendencies that strive for the mastery. The work of preparation is an individual work. We are not saved in groups. The purity and devotion of one will not offset the want of these qualities in another. Though all nations are to pass in judgment before God, yet He will examine the case of each individual with as close and searching scrutiny as if there were not another being upon the earth. Everyone must be tested and found without spot or wrinkle or any such thing.

Solemn are the scenes connected with the closing work of the atonement. Momentous are the interests involved therein. The judgment is now passing in the sanctuary above. For many years this work has been in progress. Soon—none know how soon—it will pass to the cases of the living. In the awful presence of God our lives are to come up in review. At this time above all others it behooves every soul to heed the Saviour's admonition: "Watch and pray: for ye know not when the time is." Mark 13:33. "If therefore thou shalt not watch, I will come on thee as a thief, and thou shalt not know what hour I will come upon thee." Revelation 3:3.

When the work of the investigative judgment closes, the destiny of all will have been decided for life or death. Probation is ended a short time before the appearing of the Lord in the clouds of heaven. Christ in the Revelation, looking forward to that time, declares: "He that is unjust, let him be unjust still: and he which is filthy, let him be filthy still: and he that is righteous let him be righteous still: and he that is holy, let him be holy still. And, behold, I come quickly; and My reward is with Me, to give every man according as his work shall be." Revelation 22:11, 12.

The righteous and the wicked will still be living upon the earth in their mortal state—men will be planting and building, eating and drinking, all unconscious that the final, irrevocable decision has been pronounced in the sanctuary above. Before the Flood, after Noah entered the ark, God shut him in and shut the ungodly out; but for seven days the people, knowing not that their doom was fixed, continued their careless, pleasure-loving life and mocked the warnings of impending judgment. "So," says the Saviour, "shall also the coming of the Son of man be." Matthew 24:39. Silently, unnoticed as the midnight thief, will come the decisive hour which marks the fixing of every man's destiny, the final withdrawal of mercy's offer to guilty men.

"Watch ye therefore: . . . lest coming suddenly He find you sleeping." Mark 13:35, 36. Perilous is the condition of those who, growing weary of their watch, turn to the attractions of the world. While the man of business is absorbed in the pursuit of gain, while the pleasure lover is seeking indulgence, while the daughter of fashion is arranging her adornments—it may be in that hour the Judge of all the earth will pronounce the sentence: "Thou art weighed in the balances, and art found wanting." Daniel 5:27.—*The Great Controversy*, pages 479-491.

STUDY QUESTIONS

1. What takes place at Christ's "coming" described in Daniel 7:13, 14? (115)
2. Which cases only are considered in the investigative judgment? (116)
3. Certain names only are recorded in the book of life. Who are they? (117)
4. How much does the book of remembrance contain? (117)
5. What other "record" is carefully kept? (117, 118)
6. In the investigative judgment, what *two* things happen if there are sins remaining on the books of record? (119)
7. At what time are forgiven sins blotted out—when they are forgiven, or at the final judgment? Why? (121)
8. What guilt will Satan bear? How is this fact illustrated in the Old Testament sanctuary service? (122)
9. In addition to *actions,* what other things are considered in the judgment? (123, 124)
10. How is any act we commit given value? (123)
11. Two acts of Christ have equal value in the plan of salvation. What are they? (125)
12. How does Satan "taunt" Christ and holy angels in the judgment? What does he claim it is impossible for men to do? What is the answer to this claim? (125, 126)
13. How should we use the remaining days of probation? (126, 127)